When Panthers Roared

When Panthers Roared

The Fort Worth Cats and Minor League Baseball

By Jeff Guinn with Bobby Bragan

Texas Christian University Press
Fort Worth

Library of Congress Cataloging-in-Publication Data

Guinn, Jeff.
When Panthers roared : the Fort Worth Cats and minor league baseball / by Jeff Guinn with Bobby Bragan.
p. cm
Includes index.
ISBN 0-87565-205-0 (cloth : alk. paper).—ISBN 0-87565-213-1 (pbk. : alk. paper)
1. Fort Worth Panthers (Baseball team)—History. 2. Fort Worth Cats (Baseball team)—History 3. Minor league baseball—Texas-Fort Worth—History. I. Bragan, Bobby, 1917- . II. Title.
GV875.F67G85 1999
796.357'64'097645315—dc21 99-37803
CIP

Title page photo collage of Cat memorabilia from the collection of Mark Presswood (photo by Jim Crocker).

Design: Shadetree Studio

In memory of
Pat McMillion,
who was everything
a baseball fan
should be.

1949 (Mark Presswood Collection).

Contents

Acknowledgments

Since this book is in part an oral history, it was important to find qualified baseball historians to talk about the early days of baseball, the Texas League and the Fort Worth Cats. We found two of the best: Bob Bluthardt, an officer for the Society of American Baseball Researchers (SABR), and SABR member Mark Presswood, who has spent much of his adult life corresponding with former Cats players, team officials and fans.

Former Cats players, opponents and fans were generous with their time: Harry Walker, Maury Wills, Joe Macko, Jack Lindsey, Mike Napoli, Dick Williams, Carroll Beringer, Hank Aaron, Wally Moon, Ann King Patrick and Jan King Rhinefort. Material from Joe DiMaggio, Leo Durocher and Vincent Devaney came from interviews associated with previous books and articles.

Mark Presswood generously has shared his photo and memorabilia collection with us in addition to his own opinions as a baseball historian. Comments from Barbara Feagin Stroud (Miss Fort Worth Cats 1949) are excerpted from a letter she wrote to Mark; Bill Lillard's, Williams Clark's and Herbert Bain's comments about playing for Rogers Hornsby also come from letters they exchanged with Mark.

Several fine books have served as valuable references, and we enthusiastically recommend them to anyone who wants to know about minor league baseball in general and the Texas League in particular. They include William B. Ruggles' *The History of the Texas League of Professional Baseball Clubs, 1888-1951* (now out of print, but sometimes still available through special sports bookfinders); *The Texas League: A Century of Baseball* by Bill O'Neal (Austin: Eakin Press, 1987); *The Minor League Register*, edited by Lloyd Johnson (Durham, North Carolina: Baseball America, 1994); and David Pietrusza's *Minor Miracles: The Legend & Lore of Minor League Baseball* (South Bend, Indiana: Diamond Communications, 1995).

Personal thanks go to Judy Alter, Tracy Row, Vincent Devaney's extended family, Howard Green, Judge Tom Vandergriff, Whit Canning, T.R. Sullivan (great research on Kid Nance), Sumter Bruton, Andy Grieser, Marsha Anderson, Wilson McMillion, Rich Billings, Zonk Lanzillo, Robert Fernandez, Adam and Grant Skokan-Guinn.

We're especially grateful to our wives, Nora Skokan-Guinn and Betty Bragan, who support us in all we do.

Proceeds from *When Panthers Roared* will benefit Fort Worth's Day Resource Center for the Homeless and the Bobby Bragan Youth Foundation. The Cats are still contributing to the community they loved.

Jeff Guinn
Bobby Bragan
Fort Worth, Texas

Prologue: The Remains of LaGrave

They tore down LaGrave Field in 1967. Millers Excavating was hired to obliterate the park where the legendary Fort Worth Cats of the Texas League played. The stadium was falling apart in its old nesting spot beside the Trinity River, anyway.

Parts of the ballpark were preserved and taken elsewhere. A fan named Elmer Kosob, the baseball coach and athletic director of St. Mary's University in San Antonio, had arranged to purchase some of the bleachers and the light standards. Some were sent to the ball field at St. Mary's. Several light standards were shipped to Pan American College at Edinburg (now called the University of Texas—Pan American). Another set of bleachers would soon seat fans at Marble Falls High School. No one now seems certain of where the individual box seats went, though historian-memorabilia collectors all over Texas would like to find out.

The Fort Worth Cats franchise has been gone for more than 35 years, but some of the players still live in the town they grew to love. Bobby Bragan holds court almost every morning in Fort Worth's Paris Coffee Shop. Mike Napoli, Jack Lindsey and others enjoy meeting him there to swap stories about the good old days. Carroll Beringer regularly imports old friends from the Brooklyn Dodgers-Fort Worth Cats days to be featured speakers at fund raisers he organizes for the Texas Wesleyan University baseball program. Duke Snider, Carl Erskine, Tommy Lasorda, Maury Wills, Dick Williams and Sparky Anderson have all been guests of honor on behalf of Texas Wesleyan.

The Texas League is still around, and there is also an independent Texas-Louisiana League that has stayed in business. In recent years there has even been talk of reviving the Fort Worth Cats to compete in that league, though nothing yet has come of it. There has also been discussion of rebuilding LaGrave Field, perhaps for use by the Texas Wesleyan University baseball team.

Besides, not all of LaGrave Field is gone. Anyone wandering north of downtown Fort Worth can still find the sunken remains of two dugouts and part of the tunnel that led under the old stands to the clubhouse. At just the right time of day, as afternoon blends into evening, the wind picks up and, in its whistle, there are almost echoes of cheers, of the crack of ball against bat and the sharp slap of ball meeting leather glove. It is all still there in the mind's eye, as real or even more real than the posturings of millionaire modern ballplayers 20 miles east at the Ballpark in Arlington.

Probably, if Jake Atz or Bobby Bragan could somehow resurrect their favorite teams and bring them to Arlington to challenge the Texas Rangers, the current pros would win. But if the Rangers had to come west to the remains of LaGrave, they wouldn't have an easy time of it. Compared to the Fort Worth Cats, of course, the Rangers haven't accomplished much yet. Let them win six American League pennants in a row and five out of six World Series. Then they can meet the Fort Worth Cats as equals on the Cats' home ground. But only then.

The ghosts and memories of the Cats and of LaGrave Field are waiting.

LaGrave Field at dusk in the mid-1950s (Mark Presswood Collection).

1

Baseball Comes to Texas

The game of baseball was never really invented. It evolved from other games, including cricket and towne ball played with balls, bats and bases on village greens in England and, we suppose, Britain's American colonies. The myth that Abner Doubleday created the sport in a farmer's field near Cooperstown, New York, has been thoroughly debunked. Today, even the Cooperstown Chamber of Commerce admits on its internet website that "we probably weren't the birthplace of baseball."

Baseball immortal Branch Rickey, who would become one of the major figures in the glittering history of the Fort Worth Cats, was fond of pointing out "the only thing Major General Abner Doubleday ever started was the Civil War," a snide reference to Doubleday's presence as a member of the Union garrison when the South shelled Fort Sumter on April 12, 1861. Doubleday, however, may have been the man who brought a formalized version of the sport to Texas when the United States Army sent him to Galveston in 1866 after the surrender of the Confederacy.

The game that arrived in Texas after the Civil War was already much different than the randomly ruled sport originally played as early as the 1830s. There is evidence that formal "base ball" was played in New York in 1832, and we know that Alexander Cartwright, often identified as the inventor of baseball, organized the Knickerbockers in New York City in 1842. Fans who turned out to see games were known as "kranks."

Part of that primitive game would be recognizable today. A pitcher threw a ball toward a hitter, though he probably tossed it underhand. The batter tried to hit the ball; if he succeeded, he ran to first base, second base, third base and home base in that order. The team scoring the most runs at the end of an agreed-upon time was declared the winner. But bases were approximately 75 feet—42 paces, in the jargon of the day—apart rather than 90 feet. Sometimes the pitcher stood as close to the batter as 40 feet away. Three infielders often played instead of the modern-day four; the shortstop's position was excluded. There was a "behind" rather

The 1895 Fort Worth Panthers, the city's first Texas League champions (Mark Presswood Collection).

than a "catcher." But there were often 10 or 11 men in the field, with extra players milling about the outfield. The number usually depended on how many players each team had available.

Base ball wasn't confined to New York. Other northeastern cites had their own amateur teams. The Philadelphia Olympics were especially heralded. Cartwright's Knickerbockers didn't even have their home city to themselves. Soon the New York Base Ball Club and the Brooklyn Ball Club had their own games and fans. Base ball moved as far south as Washington, D.C., where the squad was called the Gothams. By 1856, there were 12 teams in all.

All of this, though, was strictly for fun. The notion of professional sports was never involved. Even in base ball's earliest days, there was already controversy about its origins. Members of the New York Base Ball Club, for instance, insisted their team had come before Cartwright's; that, in fact, some of their members helped Cartwright get his club started. Abner Doubleday's name never came up.

Eventually Daniel "Doc" Adams, president of the Knickerbockers, was assigned the task of creating uniform rules and overseeing the founding of additional teams so leagues could be formed and official schedules played out. These rules, however, remained regional. Only when professional baseball became organized throughout the East and Midwest was one set of rules adopted for all pro and amateur teams to follow.

Alexander Cartwright worked for Adams on rules development. Henry Chadwick, yet another base ball pioneer sometimes credited with starting the game, helped as well. He even suggested not filling bases with sand, since this made them too heavy.

We know that base ball was played in Civil War campgrounds. While some variations of the game probably were played in the South before the war, it is also clear the North had the more refined, organized pastime. Historians believe this was a byproduct of the industrial North offering more free time to healthy young men. In the agrarian South, less leisure time was available to those who had to work daily in the fields.

In any event, the South eventually lost the Civil War, and Doubleday was stationed in Galveston. Post-war reconstruction tensions were high, and Doubleday and the Union troops were not made welcome by Texans. There is no way to be certain Doubleday was the organizer, but on April 21, 1867—San Jacinto Day—the first recorded base ball game in Texas was played. Significantly, the contest was between the Houston Stonewalls and the hometown Galveston R. E. Lees. Houston won 35-2. Baseball historian William B. Ruggles noted in *The History of the Texas League* that "it was years before the post-Civil War ill-feeling between Texans and [northerners] wore off." Obviously, these "ill-feelings" had their origins far from any base ball fields. Yet they would become part and parcel of regional rivalries involving the sport.

Even though they may have been introduced to its most modern form by Yankee carpetbaggers, Texans took to base ball. Four decades after the fact, *Houston Post* sportswriter John Trentem rhapsodized that first baseman Wakely Williamson of the Houston Stonewalls "could catch the swiftest thrown balls easily and gracefully, whether they were high, low, or to the side. He used his bare hands and seldom dropped a throw."

There was never a possibility Texas cities might form their own base ball clubs and play matches against squads from the northeast. Travel problems alone would have made such contests impossible. Besides, self-respecting Texans wanted to keep their favorite new sport untainted by contact with the North.

And in the North, things were happening fast. Base ball became "baseball," and the first professional teams began play.

In 1869, the Cincinnati Red Stockings fielded a squad of crack players who wanted to be paid for entertaining the kranks. This meant admission had to be charged when they took on amateur nines. Baseball rules had been formalized to the extent that there was a set number of players allowed in the lineup. Shortstop was included, the position added to make relay throws easier from the outfield to home base or plate. Catchers, no longer called behinders, sometimes fashioned rudimentary masks to protect their faces. Immediately, longtime fans who had enjoyed the play-without-pay era began to worry that their beloved sport would be corrupted.

Poet H.C. Dodge mourned in part:

Oh, don't you remember the game of base-ball we saw twenty years ago played,
When contests were true, and the sight free to all, and home-runs in plenty were made?
Now salaried pitchers who throw the ball curved at padded and masked catchers lame
And gate-money music and seats all reserved is all that is left of the game.

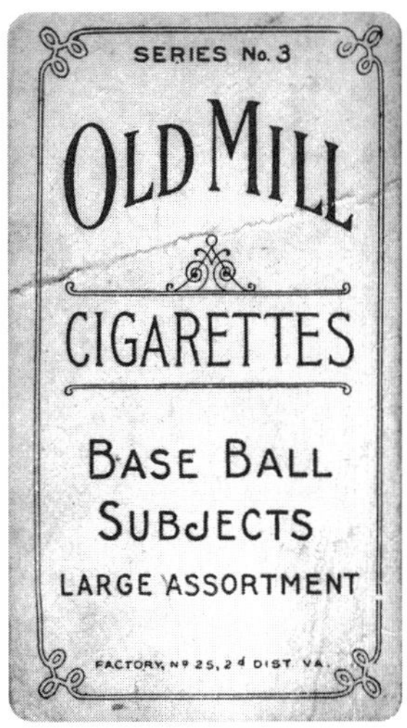

"Cigarette" card mementos, circa 1909-1911 (Mark Presswood Collection). Clockwise, from above: C.A. Deardorff, pitcher, Charles Belew, catcher, J. Walter Morris, second baseman, Ike Pendleton, outfielder.

> Oh, give us the glorious matches of old, when love of true sport made them great,
> And not this new-fashioned affair always sold for the boodle they take at the gate.

Despite Dodge and other old-timers like him, the Red Stockings were an immediate success, breaking even financially in their first season while routinely clobbering opponents whose attention to the game was necessarily diverted by the demands of fulltime jobs. Cincinnati's success was bound to attract the attention of other cities with clubs starring top amateurs who wanted to get paid for playing, too. In 1871 a full-fledged, nine-team professional baseball organization formed—the National Association of Professional Base-Ball Players. The National Association would last through the 1875 season; during that time, 23 different teams would be part of the action. These included several New York City clubs and nines from such cities as Cleveland, Philadelphia, Boston, Baltimore and Hartford. Washington, D.C., and St. Louis were as far south and west as the league cared to extend. When the National Association folded in 1875, the eight-team National League immediately came into existence. Six National Association squads, joined by teams from Cincinnati and Louisville, switched to the new league. Professional baseball remained geographically restricted. In Texas, as in the rest of the West and South, amateur players began to resent northeastern assumptions that their professional athletes were clearly superior to the farm boys playing in Dixie pastures.

Bobby Bragan:

"It never occurred to people in the South and West who loved baseball that their cities would get professional teams, major-league teams, that could take on teams from the North. It was believed this was just one more way the North was rubbing it in that they had won the [Civil] war. They believed they were sophisticated people and we were just farmers. At least this was how it was perceived in Texas and the South. The dream of early baseball fans in Texas and the South became one of hoping to see their teams knock off the loud-mouthed Yankee teams, if the Yankee teams ever showed enough gumption to come and play us."

Mark Presswood:

"Baseball was certainly better organized in the North back then. Athletes from Texas were just as physically gifted, I'm sure, as anyone from the North, but the northern players had more chances to refine their baseball skills. So, of course, overall their teams were better, though Texans would not have wanted to admit that.

"Another advantage northern teams had was that almost all of America's big cities at the time were east of the Mississippi. Sure, you had Denver and San

> Francisco and Houston, but the distance from those more scattered western cities to the relatively close eastern ones of New York, Washington and Philadelphia meant there was just no way they could all compete in one professional baseball league.
>
> "And when those (Northern) cities organized teams, they had more players to choose from. In Texas cities like Fort Worth, you might have a few men who were good players and then you'd have to surround them with other players who didn't have much experience but were willing to go out and play in front of people anyway."

If Texans needed proof their teams were overmatched, they got it in 1877 when a squad of pros from Indianapolis took on an amateur club in Galveston. The final score of the game is uncertain, but the visitors won easily. Indianapolis pitcher Edward "The Only" Nolan struck out 26 of the 27 hitters he faced. Apparently, Nolan threw a wicked curveball; Texas hitters hadn't seen many of those previously. One Galveston batter, Bill O'Neal reports in *The Texas League*, managed to dribble a weak grounder to shortstop.

While Texas continued to develop amateur teams, professional baseball spread in the industrial northeast. Several new pro leagues sprang up to challenge the National League. Most folded within a few seasons. It was 1901 before the American League was founded; while it has lasted to provide the National League with a rival, it has also always been known as the "Junior Circuit."

In 1887, though, professional baseball and Texas finally came together. It began in the fall, when three pro teams—the American Association's St. Louis Browns, the National League's New York Giants and another team made up of some Chicago players and ringers—barnstormed through Texas. Barnstorming was a convenient post-season way for professional players to make a few extra dollars. They would travel to regions of the country where no professional baseball was played and put on exhibitions, either playing each other or an area's best amateur squad. The Browns and the Chicago team played in Houston; a good crowd turned out. So far as is known, this was the first fully professional game ever played in Texas.

Another pro team was also barnstorming in Texas. This one was led by John McCloskey, a player for St. Joseph, Missouri, in the Western League. McCloskey recruited other Western League players and took a team he called the Joplin Independents to Texas.

Mark Presswood:

> "McCloskey's team played Texas exhibitions against another team made up of mostly Texas players. One game was played in Fort Worth, another in Waco and another in Austin. The New York Giants were also in Texas, and McCloskey challenged the Giants to a best-of-three series in Austin. The Giants were the real enemy as far as Texas fans were concerned. They came from New York, for one thing. There were lots of people in Austin at the time (the capitol building was about to be dedicated) this best-of-three match up occurred. Big crowds turned out for the games. McCloskey's team won the first two and the Giants left town without ever playing the third."

McCloskey was pleased by both the large turnout and the enthusiasm of the fans. He believed a professional baseball league could thrive in Texas. On December 15th and 16th, McCloskey met in Austin with business leaders from most major Texas cities to discuss the formation of a "State Base-Ball League." William H. Ward, a successful local businessman, represented Fort Worth.

2

The Birth of the Texas League

The fledgling Texas League was not the first in the state, or even the first to bear that name. In 1884, a mostly amateur "Texas League" was formed with teams from Houston, Fort Worth, Galveston, Dallas and Waco. Samuel L. Hain, who had played semi-pro baseball back east, was the organizer. In the same year, baseball also came to Texas colleges. The University of Texas Longhorns and the Aggies of Texas A&M (then called the Agricultural and Mechanical College) had the first meeting in a baseball rivalry that continues to this day.

Amateur clubs from Texas cities had been competing for years. Fort Worth fielded some of the very earliest teams.

Mark Presswood:

> "To put things in perspective, when the first team named the Fort Worth Panthers began to play, Butch Cassidy and the Sundance Kid were still roaming the West. The first account I know of concerning a Fort Worth team came in 1879 when it traveled to a game in Houston by buckboard. Some people say it took them a week to get there; others say it took two weeks. Either way, it was a long, hot, rugged ride."

That first Fort Worth team was called the Panthers in honor of its hometown. Fort Worth was supposedly such a quiet place that a panther was once seen sleeping in the town square. This is surely an apocryphal tale invented by a visitor from Dallas, but the nickname stuck.

McCloskey and his professional baseball partners set out in December 1887 to start a new league that would be strictly professional. Fans all over Texas, McCloskey felt certain, would pay to see top-flight baseball. The thrashings suffered in Austin by the despised New York Giants had "aroused the sporting blood of the... population," he insisted.

The league organizers set ground rules. Teams would be placed in Austin, Dallas, Houston, Fort Worth, Galveston and New Orleans. Fred Turner, a businessman from Austin, was elected league president; teams were allowed a total of $1,000 each per season to pay the salaries of their entire rosters. But by the second league meeting in January 1888, things were already changing. Team organizers in New Orleans decided to join another new league. San Antonio was invited into the Texas League to replace them. A company was hired to manufacture official Texas League baseballs. Admission prices were the subject of heated debate; eventually, it was agreed that game tickets would be priced at 25 cents. The league's first games would be played on April 5.

Things were off-kilter from the start. Turner decided he wasn't interested in being league president, something he had perceived more as a figurehead position than a real job. Houston's Robert Adair (probably an investor in the Houston Buffs), who had initially been tapped as Texas League vice-president, stepped in. He had his work cut out for him. A league schedule wasn't finalized and play didn't begin until April 8th. Some teams had trouble filling 13-to-17 player rosters with enough actual professionals. Austin, led by McCloskey, had the easiest method of putting a club together. McCloskey simply moved most of his Joplin barnstormers to Texas.

Play in the Texas League's first season was primitive. Teams had trouble just getting to away games. When games were scheduled in cities like Fort Worth and Dallas, it was possible for visiting teams to travel by train. Sometimes, though, buckboards were still the conveyance of necessity if not choice. Pitchers stood 50 feet away from batters. They were allowed by league rules to throw overhand, but many still used the old underhand method. Baseballs were scarce at some games; if one was fouled into the stands or, infrequently, blasted completely out of the park, action stopped so the ball could be retrieved. Night baseball was unknown. Games were played in the afternoon, and though their pace was quicker than modern baseball—for one thing, starting pitchers were expected to last the whole game—it wasn't uncommon for final innings to be played in twilight when neither players nor spectators could really see the ball.

Bobby Bragan:

> "They didn't have gloves then; they played with their bare hands. The players were taught to catch with both hands. Those who did try to protect their hands did so by wearing ordinary work gloves, the kind anyone could buy in general stores. They would cut off the tips of the fingers on the gloves so they could feel the ball, grip it better. Bats were often crafted by the players themselves; you took a good piece

of wood and shaped it. If your bat cracked, you tried to tape or nail it back together.

"Players who were injured didn't get paid if they didn't play. Salaries were very low, so if you could walk onto the field you played."

Mark Presswood:

"The idea in the Texas League was always to have totally professional teams, but it just wasn't possible a lot of the time. Players might jump from one team to another if they got a few more dollars from the owner of the new team. There were actually times in the first few seasons of the Texas League when teams had to call people out of the stands to play, or go to a local high school before the games and recruit some players there.

Bobby Bragan

"A lot of the so-called equipment was a joke. Catchers tried to use some kind of mask (often fashoned from chicken wire) because that let them be closer to the batter. The reason they wanted to be closer was to have a shorter throw to second base if somebody tried to steal. And all the players had trouble with traction on the field. There were no cleats. They all wore slick-soled shoes. At least their caps usually had little bills in front to help block out the sun."

Despite McCloskey's hopes, many Texans weren't ready to pay good money to watch baseball games. Thirty-three games into the 1888 season, San Antonio dropped out of the Texas League early in June with a 6-27 record. With only five teams left, it was impossible to follow the original league schedule. Whatever team didn't play on a given day lost gate receipts that were desperately needed. But because of the scheduling problems, and because quick transportation between league cities wasn't always available, teams might go the better part of a week without playing at all.

Some cities were rumored to be ready to step in and replace San Antonio. Waco, Temple and Texarkana apparently wanted Texas League franchises. The league was ready to accept any or all of them. If a city's business leaders could show sufficient financial wherewithal to support a team through a full season, they would be welcome to join. In this case, there were more applicants than places available; to fulfill the original schedule, just one new team could be added. But before any decision could be made about which applicant to approve, the Fort Worth Panthers also disbanded. They had struggled to a 19-25 mark. Fort Worth fans weren't interested in supporting a loser.

Instead of adding new teams, the Texas League suddenly couldn't even sustain the four it still had. Shockingly, Austinites stopped turning out to watch McCloskey's team play. He eventually moved the club to San Antonio in mid-season. Desperate, league officials agreed to let New Orleans come into the league after all; again, a five-team format proved awkward. Though the 1888 season was supposed to run through October, in September Houston and Galveston dropped out. New Orleans owners thought the Texas League was done for and pulled out, too. Only Dallas and San Antonio were left. The league terminated its first season on September 2. Owners of the Dallas Hams then demonstrated why theirs had been the only club able to enjoy reasonably solid financial footing; instead of being dismayed by the early, unscheduled end of the Texas League season, they took their team off on a barnstorming tour of Midwest cities.

Because the season had ended prematurely, the league didn't proclaim a pennant winner for 1888. McCloskey argued that his San Antonio team ought to share the honor with Dallas, but nothing came of it. Dallas had the best team record at 55-27. Austin/San Antonio finished 38-29.

Bobby Bragan:

> "I'm sure there was never really any serious discussion of throwing in the towel on the league after 1888. Maybe some things hadn't worked out as planned, but across the country everyone still loved baseball. The Texas League people had to think of ways to make more fans want to come to the ballparks and pay to see games. Most professional baseball leagues struggled in the beginning. If you look at the National Association—the National League—they had teams drop out all the time."

1920 Southern Championship—Fort Worth versus Little Rock (Bobby Bragan Collection).

Bob Bluthardt:

> "Growing pains were very much a part of all professional baseball leagues at this time. The owners of most so-called minor-league clubs, including those in the Texas League, were community-based folks who saw owning and operating teams as an extension of their civic responsibility."

In January 1889, Texas League organizers met again, this time in Fort Worth. For the league's second season, there would be six teams—Austin, Dallas, Fort Worth, Galveston, Houston and Waco. Unhappy with the way Austin kranks had failed to support his team in 1888, McCloskey took the nucleus of that club to Houston, nicknaming them the "Babies."

Most of those attending the winter meeting felt reasonably optimistic. Dallas had proven a Texas league club could last an entire season. Several players who found themselves unemployed when their Texas League teams folded had been able to catch on in other leagues, playing quite well and, at least in the minds of the Texas League movers and shakers, proving the level of Texas League play was as good as any other league had to offer. The Texas League was already earning a reputation as a "dead ball" league where the official ball was impossible to hit very hard or very far. Historian Bill O'Neal points out the term "Texas leaguer," used to describe a bloop hit, was coined in 1888 when ex-Texas League standout Harry Raymond went on to play for Louisville and make his way on base with a series of soft fly balls that barely eluded scampering infielders.

In 1889, the Texas League did a little better. Its season still came to a premature end, but McCloskey's Houston Babies dominated throughout and were awarded the league's first official pennant. All the franchises, though, ran into financial problems. Surprisingly, Dallas was the first to toss in the money towel. On June 2 its owners announced they would disband the club, but enough cash was raised the next day to keep it going. In August the league fell apart. Houston and Austin quit first, followed in order by Dallas, Galveston, Fort Worth and Waco. But a longer season had been achieved. That was also the first season league executives attempted to keep official batting and earned-run averages. A third season, they believed, would finally see the completion of a full schedule.

The same six Texas League teams began the 1890 season. It was a disaster. Austin and Fort Worth claimed to have hired the same man, veteran pro ballplayer Harry Truby. Austin thought Truby was its manager, and Fort Worth considered him a player on its active roster. Eventually the league wouldn't let either club have him, and Austin had to begin its season without a manager. While this proved awkward for Austin, it did demonstrate that when Texas League officials made rulings, Texas League franchises had to obey.

Except for Galveston, most of the clubs lost as many games as they won. Fans stopped coming to the ballparks. The entire league closed down barely two months into the season. McCloskey took many of the best players in the league and formed a team in California. In 1891, there was no Texas League season at all. Apparently, professional baseball was finished in the state. Chronicler William B. Ruggles suggests that "three successive failures evidentally put a dampener on the sporting spirit of Texas baseball backers."

Mark Presswood:

> "A lot of the problem was that too many Texas League cities had up-and-down economies. Fort Worth was dependent on agriculture and solid farm prices. If that slumped, people couldn't afford to go to ballgames. You'll notice the most successful teams in the early Texas League were the southern Texas cities—Houston, Galveston. The financial strength of the state was in that region. It was always the north and central Texas teams that folded first.
>
> "The key to this era in the Texas League was that there was no structure to it. Everything was by the seat of the pants."

The Texas League re-formed in 1892, shut down again until 1895, lasted through 1899 and took another sabbatical until 1902. From 1903 to 1906 the league split into the North Texas League and South Texas League, each with four franchises. In all, the league disbanded three times in its first 20 years of existence. But it kept coming back.

Bobby Bragan:

> "Baseball was *the* game. It was the best type of entertainment available. Better structure was necessary in those early days. This was obvious. But also obvious was that people needed someplace to go, something to watch. Baseball even then was a game easy to watch and understand. Kids could imagine themselves playing it. A quarter for a ticket was steep in those days, but not so expensive most people couldn't afford it. The idea of professional sports was still new. I never think it became a matter of if professional baseball would catch on in Texas, but when. People like William Ward in Fort Worth didn't give up easily."

One significant event occurred in 1901 when the National Association of Professional Baseball Leagues was formed as an umbrella organization for pro leagues which were not recognized, like the National and American leagues, as "major" or top of the professional ladder. The NAPBL set out to standardize rules, matching them to major-league regulations—placing all pitchers 60 feet, six inches away from the batter, for instance—and eliminating contractual loopholes that allowed the best minor-league players to jump from one team to another at will.

Further, America was developing much more of a national identity. Other sports, from boxing to cricket to horse racing to track and field, were clearly the creations of other countries. Baseball was American.

America's regional antagonisms, dating back to the Civil War, were still very much in place. Promotors in southern and western minor leagues eventually realized one way to gain community support was to play off the "them versus us" theme. The two major leagues consisted entirely of north and northeastern teams and cities. When major-league teams began taking spring training in or barnstorming through Texas—John McGraw's New York Giants trained in Marlin near Waco because McGraw liked bathing in mineral water spas there—Texas fans had chances to see suddenly beloved local teams take on the hated Yankees. (It also helped that New York's American League team eventually adopted "Yankees" as its nickname in the early 1900s.)

Bobby Bragan:

"You bet Texas League team owners used that. All of us from the South just hated the North. They called their leagues the major leagues and we had the minor leagues. We took it as one more way they were saying they were better than us. When I was a boy growing up in Birmingham, I got to see Babe Ruth play in an exhibition game. I was excited to see Ruth, but I wanted our team to beat him and his northern friends."

The Texas League eventually joined the NAPBL, bringing some stability to its rules. After a few more false starts, the association managed to complete season schedules and become a stable presence. By the 1920s, in fact, it was one of the more famous minor leagues in the country.

That was largely because of the Fort Worth Panthers, a team all American baseball fans suddenly knew and talked about.

3

The Early Panthers

The Fort Worth Panthers were not an instant success; like every other fledgling Texas League franchise, the Cats struggled at the box office. Besides the vagaries of the North Texas economy, their chances for winning the hearts of local fans were reduced because the first few incarnations of the Fort Worth Panthers were simply bad baseball teams.

"Big Mike" O'Connor, who'd been one of the better players opposing McCloskey's Joplin squad on their 1887 Texas barnstorming tour, was named the Panthers' first manager. Team owner William Ward could help out most by encouraging other Fort Worth business leaders to support the team financially. But, with a league-mandated salary cap of $1,000 for the entire Fort Worth roster, Ward couldn't spend additional money to bring better, higher-salaried players to the roster after it became clear the players they did have weren't going to win many games.

The best player on the first Panthers team was probably Bill "Scrappy" Joyce, who went on from the Texas League to play for several major league clubs and eventually manage the New York Giants. But Joyce and O'Connor weren't enough; the Panthers folded in June. The team's 19-25 record was an accurate reflection of its talent.

O'Connor got out while the getting was good; J.M. Horsfield became the Panthers' second manager. His 1889 Fort Worth club played further into the season but had a losing record of 45-51 when they shut down in mid-August. O'Connor was lured back to play first base in 1890, but the Panthers still lost. Fort Worth shut down in early June, and the Texas League itself was finished on June 10th. The Texas League seemed very much the clone of dozens of other minor leagues around the country. Americans obviously loved baseball, but except for the northeast it seemed not enough people loved it sufficiently to pay to see games.

Mark Presswood:

"Even in the tough early days, the Fort Worth franchise had a lot going for it. W. H. Ward was a solid businessman and promotor. His continuing involvement with the team meant there would be quite a few chances for the Panthers to catch on. The ballpark where the Panthers played, a 1,200-seat stadium just south of the T&P railway station, was as good as any in the league. What had to happen to make the Panthers a success was for them to have enough winning seasons to win over the fans. Once that happened, the Panthers were going to be set."

Bobby Bragan:

"Whether in 1889 or 1999, fans will support a team that wins. It doesn't have to win all the time, but the fans have to believe that every few seasons the team they're supporting will have a chance to win it all. The early Cats teams were bad. Fort Worth was a prairie city. Many people had farms to tend, constant chores to see to.

"In those early years, too, Fort Worth did not have a player or manager who was so outstanding people would pay just to see him, even if his team lost more than it won. A good major-league comparison would be Ernie Banks with those terrible Chicago Cubs teams in the late 1950s and early 1960s. You would go to Wrigley Field knowing the Cubs would probably lose, but you would have the pleasure of watching Ernie Banks."

Somehow, the Panthers survived over the next decade or so. There were times when Ward relinquished control of the team, but he was usually involved in some capacity.

When the league geared up for the third time in 1895, Panthers fans finally found they had a quality team to support.

Mark Presswood:

"The Cats' first championship was awarded in 1895. At this time, the Texas League had no established playoff criteria. The season was generally broken into two halves, and the winners of each half met in the post-season to determine the season champion. This was partly to keep up fan interest through the entire summer and early fall. If your team did badly in the first half, it might improve a lot in the second half and still have a shot at winning the championship. Quite a few times, though, the post-season championship never happened because the two teams involved couldn't agree on how and when to get together. Also, at the end of the regular season lots of players had to leave their teams right away to start full-time off-season jobs. They didn't make enough money during the baseball season to live on over the winter. Finally, lots of times the two so-called champions rebuilt their rosters for the playoff with good players from other teams. It was really a mess.

"But in 1895, the teams in the playoff were to be Dallas and Fort Worth, which was great for the league because of the rivalry between those cities. Ted Sullivan was running the Dallas team. W. H. Ward, of course, had Fort Worth. The two of them

> agreed to a best-of-fifteen playoff format. If that seems like a lot of games, you have to remember they were going to try and get every penny they could out of the series. With it being a Dallas-Fort Worth match up, they believed or maybe just hoped fans from both cities would just keep turning out.
>
> "The first game of the playoff was scheduled in Dallas. But it rained that day in Fort Worth. Ward saw the weather and decided it wouldn't be necessary for his team to make the two-hour trip. As it happened, maybe the rain wasn't as bad in Dallas. Thompson thought the game should have been played. They picked it up and started playing the next day.
>
> "After thirteen games, Fort Worth led 7-6. The fourteenth game was set for Fort Worth and the fifteenth for Dallas, but Sullivan argued his team had lost the advantage of hosting the first game and he wanted both of the last two played in Dallas. Ward wouldn't do it. Sullivan wouldn't give in, either, and the last two games never got played. Sullivan and Ward argued back and forth in the newspaper about which team should be declared the 1895 season champion, and eventually at the league's winter meetings Fort Worth was named the pennant winner."

Fort Worth's record in 1895 was a sparkling 77-39, second only to Dallas' 82-33. The Panthers also had their first big stars. Al McFarland posted a 34-12 record—no Texas League pitcher has ever won more games in a single season. Cassie McAlister hit .351, and, usually pitching when McFarland didn't, won 22 games as well.

Another player who had a brief tour with Fort Worth was William G. "Kid" Nance, who became the first major-league player from the area. Nance was just 19 in 1895; he'd signed with the Panthers right after graduating from high school. Nance didn't stay long; he jumped to the new Texas League team in Sherman, though he played part of the 1896 with the Panthers, too. Nance went on to play for the Louisville Colonels in the National League and the American League's Detroit Tigers. He lasted just one season with the Tigers, though he hit .280 as a starter in the outfield. Eventually Texas Christian University hired Nance as its baseball coach, and he also would manage the Panthers for portions of the 1913, 1914 and 1915 seasons.

Fort Worth baseball fans still weren't completely won over. The Panthers posted the best Texas League season record in 1896, going 71-29. They dominated the first half of the season, finishing it comfortably ahead of Houston. But the entire league's fortunes waned during the second half of the season; once again, clubs began folding by August. The Panthers were one of them.

The 1904 team finished first in the regular season but lost in the playoffs (Mark Presswood Collection).

Bobby Bragan:

> "I admit I've never understood why the Panthers didn't make it through that full [1896] season. I guess the Fort Worth economy must have been having its troubles."

The Panthers got through most of the 1897 season, managing to win exactly half the 100 games they played. In 1898, Fort Worth was 9-10 when the entire Texas League season was shut down after just a month of play. Historian Ruggles blames the Spanish-American War, writing "the state was simply not interested [in baseball] while troops were mobilizing."

In 1889, the Texas League was restricted to four teams from the southern part of the state. It still shut down halfway through its truncated schedule. For the next two years, neither the Panthers nor the Texas League officially existed. In the winter of 1901, enough interested parties gathered, however, to plan a 1902 season. The Panthers would return, though their old Dallas nemesis, Ted Sullivan, would run the team.

The 1902 Cats were dismal, winning 48 games and losing 62. After the season, Ward returned to head the club; as a consolation, Sullivan was offered the chance to put together another Texas franchise. He located it in Paris, which was enjoying new, short-lived prosperity from nearby oil strikes. The Texas League itself was broken in half. Northern clubs included Fort Worth, Paris (Waco in the second half of the season), Dallas and Corsicana; they represented the "official" Texas League. San Antonio, Houston, Galveston and Beaumont declared themselves the South Texas League. They stocked their rosters with many good players lured from North Texas rivals.

Even with just half the normal competition, the Cats still lost more than they won in 1903. Their team fortunes, at least on the field, changed radically in 1904, when they won their second Texas League championship. Perhaps they were inspired by the new Panther Park built by W.H. Ward.

Mark Presswood:

> "[Ward] moved the team a little to the East, to Hayne Park, which is special in Fort Worth history. In 1889 Fort Worth built a complex called the Spring Palace to host events similar to today's big stock shows. People came to the palace from all over the country. But it caught fire and a fireman named Al Hayne died fighting the blaze. So the nearby park was named in his honor. They put up his statue, too.

"This Panther Park had wooden stands with very little cover from the sun. The comfort of those being seated wasn't considered quite as important then. Admission to the games was 50 cents. Later, in 1911, J. Walter Morris built another Panther Park on North Main between 6th and 7th Streets.

"The Panthers weren't the only professional baseball team in town. The Fort Worth Yellowjackets played in what they then called a negro league, more semi-pro than completely professional. There was another black team in Dallas. Eventually the Yellowjackets renamed themselves the Fort Worth Wonders. Their league had teams from Texas, Oklahoma, Arkansas and Louisiana; it was known as the Tex-Ok-La League. In the 1920s when the Negro National League was formed, one with teams in bigger, major-league cities, all the best players from the Tex-Ok-La League left to join up there, and the smaller regional league became a minor league.

"The Cats had talent and won the Texas League championships in 1904, 1905 and 1906. But there was no real consistency of play. With just four teams in the Northern League and four in the South, there weren't enough clubs to play each other and provide the fans with much variety. The Panthers always had Dallas as a traditional rival, but otherwise in these years they'd be playing Cleburne or Paris or sometimes Corsicana was in the mix. The big Texas cities, the ones Fort Worth fans really wanted their teams to beat besides Dallas, were in the South."

Crowds in other league cities weren't as sportsmanlike as those usually found at Panther Park. When smaller towns, flush with temporary oil money, joined the Texas League, Fort Worth players sometimes found being the visiting team got dangerous.

Mark Presswood:

"There was one time in particular, either in 1902 or 1903, when Fort Worth went out to play Cleburne. Cleburne wouldn't last very long in the Texas League, but this season they had a pretty good team. The town just swelled up with pride. As the story goes, the Cats went down there to play them, and after a while had a 2-0 lead in the late innings. The crowd was rough. Some 300-400 real cowboys were even watching the game on horseback, grazing their horses out behind the outfielders. Among 'em were quite a few who were wearing their six-shooters. Cleburne tied the game 2-2 in the bottom of the ninth. They had the winning run on third base with two outs. The next Cleburne hitter popped a soft fly to centerfield, but the ball never came down to the Cats centerfielder who was waiting to catch it. About five cowboys yanked out their pistols and shot the ball out of the air. The umpire was smart enough to go ahead and award the winning run to Cleburne."

In 1907, professional teams in both the north and south of Texas re-formed the Texas League with eight franchises. In recognition, the NAPBL elevated the league classification. Under association rules, minor leagues were classified as either AAA, AA, A, B, C, D or E. Ratings depended on population of cities in the league, not the quality of play. This would gradually evolve, particularly when major-league clubs began affiliating themselves with clubs in several minor leagues and using these newly minted "farm teams" as training grounds for future major leaguers.

Prior to 1907, the Texas League had been recognized as a "D" league. But the population of the league's southern cities, plus the continued growth of Fort Worth and Dallas, earned the league a "C" rating when it was re-organized.

The 1907 season was successful for the league, but not for the Panthers. They finished fifth out of eight teams, and then fifth again in 1908. Pitchers dominated batters; there were five Texas League no-hitters in 1908. William H. Ward stuck with the Panthers for one more season; after the Cats fell to sixth in 1909 he sold his interest in the team to J. Walter Morris of Fort Worth and Waxahachie's Frank Weaver, both of whom had enjoyed enough business success to take on the risky challenge of operating a Texas League club. Morris named himself both the team's president and its manager. He had the baseball background for both jobs, having played in the Texas League for several seasons.

Almost immediately, Morris made baseball history. Before the official opening of the 1910 season, John McGraw brought his National League New York Giants to Fort Worth for an exhibition game against the Panthers. Rain first interrupted play, then cancelled it. As was the custom, fans were instructed to line up for refunds. Morris caught several getting their money back, then sneaking to the rear of the refund line in successful attempts to double-dip. Angered, he came up with the idea of issuing "rain checks" to ticketholders as they entered his ballpark. Then, in the event of rainouts, they would have to turn over these rain checks to receive refunds. Soon, every team in the league was following suit, and then all the other leagues, too.

The 1910 pennant race was tight; Dallas and Houston eventually emerged as the best teams, but Fort Worth finished a solid fourth with a 75-63 record. The Texas League routinely played full seasons now, though some clubs still had money troubles and had to be replaced from time to time.

In Fort Worth, as in other western and southern cities whose fans began to show long-term loyalty to their teams, players became local celebrities.

Baseball pioneers: Paul LaGrave, J. Walter Morris and Tony Thebo were teammates on the 1905 San Antonio Broncos (Mark Presswood Collection).

Bob Bluthardt:

"When you talk about the 1910s, you are talking about a limited media market. Newspapers could carry wire photos, but by and large most newspapers had a local focus. Radio was only about to be in its infancy. So papers often fed off the local sports scene. If you lived in Fort Worth, it was certainly more important for you to know on a daily basis how your Panthers were doing than who was leading the National League. To an extent, you might even assume the Fort Worth team was better than whatever team was leading the National League.

"You must remember that Texans had their opportunities to see major league clubs. But they didn't see them that often, or in circumstances when the major leaguers necessarily were going all-out. If a major-league club like the New York Giants barnstormed and played a dozen games against Texas League teams that were quite competent, then the major leaguers would occasionally lose a game. One of the charms of baseball is that, perhaps three or four times out of ten, even a clearly lesser team can beat a better one. When the Panthers, playing at home, beat a visiting major-league team, for the major leaguers it was just one spring game that didn't count in any standings. For the Fort Worth fans, it was absolute proof their team was just as good as the major-league club and probably better."

Bobby Bragan:

"These were still the days when minor-league teams were what we called 'independents.' They didn't belong to any major-league team. They operated themselves. The major-league teams didn't have formal scouting systems set up, so these barnstorm or exhibition games were the best chances minor-league players got to show off to major-league managers what they could do. I suspect that's one reason the minor-league teams always did so well, why they won some of the games—their players were killing themselves to impress the major-league team's manager, and his players were just trying to get into shape for the season."

Bob Bluthardt:

"At the end of the minor-league's season, team owners might then sell the contracts of one or two of their best players to a major-league team. This might be the best way for those owners to keep from losing money. Most minor-league teams were operated in farm cultures and communities, so this was the baseball equivalent of cashing in your crop at the end of harvest."

When towns like Fort Worth took their players into their hearts, the gesture went beyond cheering for them at Panther Park. Many players found relatively cushy off-season jobs in Fort Worth; often, they would stay on permanently when their playing days were over. Several Panthers owners and managers complained Fort Worth was making their players a little too comfortable. The city hadn't entirely shed the accoutrements that had made it a legend of the old wild West. Its taverns always welcomed Panthers players.

Vincent Devaney:

> "When I pitched for the Cats, I don't know that I ever had to pay for a beer."

Around the 1910 season, as local newspapers began carrying more stories about the Fort Worth team's victories and travails, writers didn't always refer to the club as the Panthers. More and more often, they wrote about "the Kittens" or "the Cats." The latter stuck even though the official name remained the Panthers. There is no record of when the franchise officially switched to the more common name. After World War II, the team's jerseys finally had "Cats" in script across the chest.

Even if they were deluding themselves about the Cats' ability to compete against major-league teams, Fort Worth fans, and fans throughout the Texas League, were finally getting their money's worth for a 50-cent ticket.

Bobby Bragan:

> "Don't kid yourself. This was not minor-league baseball like we see today, with very young kids learning the absolute basics, if that, before being rushed to the major leagues. When the Fort Worth Cats and the Texas League really got going in 1910 and thereafter, I would say the average player's age was 26 or 27. They knew how to play. Most probably had five or six years' professional experience. You knew going into professional baseball for a living that there were only 16 major-league ball clubs. Making a good minor-league club like the Cats, getting into the regular starting lineup, was, for a lot of these players, as high as they could expect to go.
>
> "Of course the Cats players all wanted to prove they could make it in the big leagues. It was every guy's ultimate dream. Then as now, after a while most dreams got tempered by reality. A guy playing for Dallas might hit 50 home runs, but after a while he probably realized he couldn't hit the fastball up in the strike zone, and that major-league pitchers could put the ball where he couldn't hit it all day long. So settling for a playing career in a city like Fort Worth was not the worst thing these players could do. Most had no education beyond high school, anyway. Fort Worth would look out for its Cats, even when they were no longer young enough to play."

Morris owned and managed the Cats until partway through the 1913 season, when Kid Nance was hired to run the club. The team only contended for the Texas League pennant once—in 1911—during Morris' tenure as manager. Before the 1914 season, Morris sold control of the team to Weaver, his partner, for $50,000. The colossal sum was proof the Fort Worth team had established itself.

Since Fort Worth, like other Texas League franchises, changed managers nearly as often as its fans changed socks, it didn't seem important when, partway through the 1914 season, Nance was replaced. The new Fort Worth manager had been an undistinguished major-league infielder for four seasons. In his only other season as a manager, during 1911 with Providence of the Eastern League, he'd led his team to a dismal 39-69 record and a last-place finish.

But Jake Atz would do much, much better with the Fort Worth Cats.

Cats manager Jake Atz watches the action from the dugout, early 1920s (Mark Presswood Collection, courtesy of San Antonio Light).

4
Atz's Cats

Somewhere along the way, Jacob Zimmerman changed his name to Jake Atz. Where it happened is a matter of dispute. Some versions have Zimmerman at the end of an Army pay line, another among a line of pro players waiting in alphabetical order to get paychecks. In both instances, the story has Zimmerman getting stiffed when money ran out before his turn. So he changed his name to Atz so he'd always be at the head of the line instead.

We do know for certain that Atz was born in Washington, D.C., in 1879. Like many boys of his day, he was fascinated by the new game of base ball and learned how to play. By 1902, having already assumed his new last name, Atz got his first taste of the major leagues with Washington. It was a brief taste; 10 at bats and just one hit later, the young second baseman was back in the minors.

It took Jake Atz five seasons to get another shot at the big leagues. This time he stuck with the Chicago White Sox for three seasons, but his batting average never got above the mid-.230s. Atz was a scrappy kid who'd do anything to get on base; but when he stepped into a pitch from legendary fastballer Walter Johnson, the resulting hip injury put Atz out of the big leagues for good.

Atz still loved baseball and wanted to be part of it. His first try at managing in 1911 with Providence turned out as badly as his major league playing career. Still, he had a reputation as a smart baseball man, and in July of 1914 Walter Morris decided Atz might have a better chance than Kid Nance to lead the Cats out of their season-long doldrums. Atz didn't; under his guidance, Fort Worth only managed to win 29 of its remaining 63 games.

Nance began the 1915 season at the Panther helm. With Fort Worth struggling around .500 in mid-June, Atz was summoned again. This time he guided the Cats to more wins than losses; they went 50-41 for him and finished third in the league.

Frank Weaver—now in control of the franchise—kept Atz on for the 1916 season. Like his predecessor Morris, Weaver believed he knew enough about baseball to run the Cats himself. Halfway through the 1916 schedule, the Cats played a home game in which their starting pitcher was hammered by opposing hitters. Weaver expected his manager to pull the struggling hurler. Atz left him in the game. Weaver started shouting for a substitution. Atz ignored him. Furious, Weaver stormed out on the field and yanked the pitcher himself. Equally furious, Atz resigned as Fort Worth's manager. He was replaced on the spot by Otto McIver.

Mark Presswood:

"By that time, J. Walter Morris had been elected president of the Texas League. He was disgusted with what Weaver had done and began hunting around for someone new to buy the Cats from Weaver and assume team ownership. Will Stripling, a Fort Worth businessman, was Morris' choice, and Stripling said he would only be interested if Morris would find him a smart business manager to handle the team finances and day-to-day operations. Morris put Stripling in touch with Paul LaGrave.

"Paul LaGrave was born in Missouri. He grew up in St. Louis and turned out to be a pretty good baseball player. He turned pro and from 1903 through 1905 was the third baseman for the San Antonio Broncos in the Texas League. That's where he met J. Walter Morris, who was a teammate. LaGrave went on to play minor-league ball for a number of other clubs, including ones in Greenville, Mississippi, and Helena, Arkansas. He even managed a team in Fort Smith. When Morris and Frank Weaver originally took over the Cats, Morris hired LaGrave to work for them. He wasn't in any decision-making capacity then. Morris felt like he knew enough baseball to run the team himself.

"But he didn't have the same kind of faith in Frank Weaver, particularly when Weaver humiliated Jake Atz like that. So when Morris was asked by Stripling to recommend a good baseball man, he was eager to tell him about Paul LaGrave."

LaGrave was, by all accounts, something of a baseball genius. What he didn't know about the game before joining the Fort Worth club, he learned faster than anyone would have thought possible. Within months, LaGrave had established a nationwide network of baseball-savvy friends who helped him track down the best professional players not under contract to major-league franchises. He never raided other minor-league clubs, but he was always ready to snap up quality performers whenever they were legally available. Perhaps his best acquisition, though, was the manager he believed Weaver should never have let get away. In 1917, Jake

Atz was back in the Fort Worth dugout, and he stayed there for most of the next 13 seasons.

Bobby Bragan:

> "Jake Atz was a great manager; to me, he was in every way the equal of the wonderful Connie Mack of the Philadelphia A's. Atz was a smart baseball man who could teach his players how the game was played, and a man who was tough enough to make them listen to him. He had a great advantage in that Paul LaGrave made certain the best Cats players stayed with the team. Atz never had to start from scratch at the beginning of a season. He had his nucleus and could build around it."

World War I was underway, but the 1917 Texas League season wasn't affected. The Cats finished in second place, trailing Texas League champion Dallas by 5½ games.

By 1919, however, the war forced a shortened schedule. But the 1919 season also gave the first indication that the Stripling-LaGrave-Atz troika was up to something special. LaGrave used his informal scouting network to bring some outstanding players to Panther Park. Perhaps foremost among them was a blocky first baseman named Clarence Kraft, nicknamed "Big Boy" and an instant fan favorite. Kraft had enjoyed only the briefest of major-league careers, three at bats in 1914 with the Boston Braves in the National League. During his seven seasons with the Cats, Kraft set Texas League batting records that stood for four decades; one, his 196 RBI total in 1924, has never been broken. He was the heart of a powerful, speedy offense that eventually included outfielder Ziggy Sears, a hitting machine with a consistent .300 batting average; Dugan Phelan, who had more major-league experience than most Texas League players combined; Bobby Stow, the shortstop who boasted no man alive could field better than he; and catcher Possum Moore, who owed his nickname to a strong facial resemblence to that creature.

As good as the Panther hitters were, the team's pitchers may have been better. Lefty Joe Pate won a minimum of 20 games five times during the Cats' amazing 1919-1925 championship run; in two of those seasons, he won 30. Right-hander Paul Wachtel complemented Pate with six 20-win seasons of his own. Unlike Pate, who eventually made it to the majors, Wachtel was resigned to a minor-league career. His best pitch was a spitball, which had been outlawed in the National and American leagues but not in Texas.

Cats fans took these colorful players to their hearts. Shreveport won the first half of the 1919 season, with the Cats in second place. Fort Worth

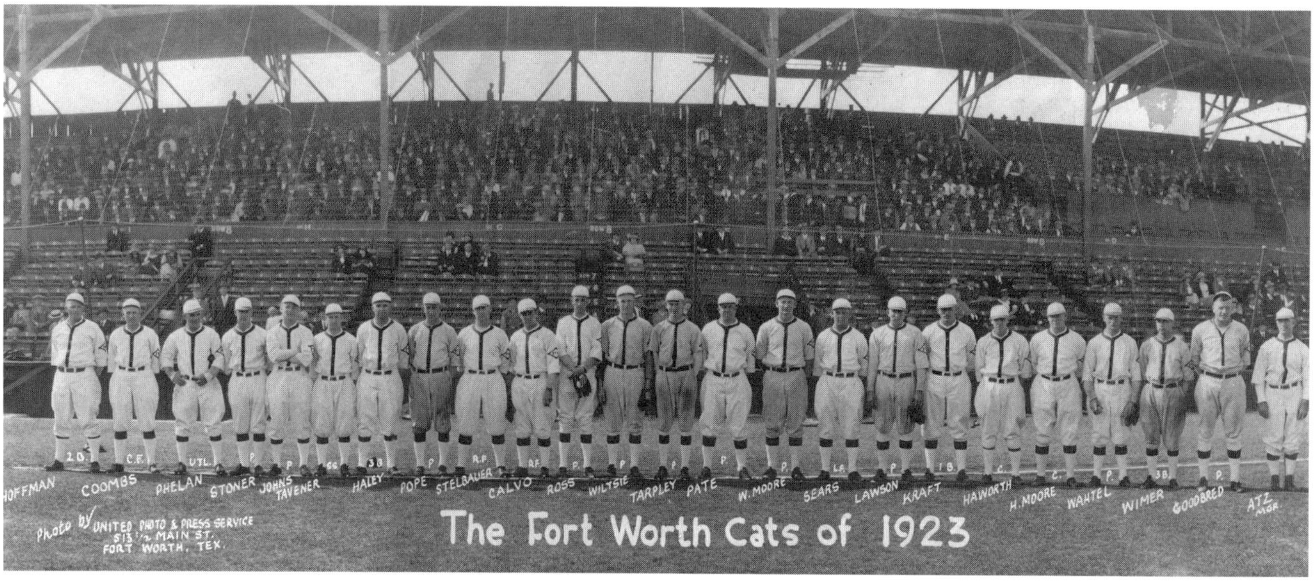

Panoramic view of the 1923 Fort Worth Panthers taken at Panther Park; the team won the Texas League pennant under the guidance of manager Jake Atz (Mark Presswood Collection).

1946 (Mark Presswood Collection).

edged Houston for the second half title and met Shreveport in a best-of-seven series to determine the 1919 Texas League champs. Shreveport won the first three games; the Cats came back to win the next two. Game six ended in a 2-2 tie; Shreveport won the seventh game, and the league title, when Fort Worth lost 6-5.

It was the last time for six seasons that the Cats would finish second in their league to anyone.

Bobby Bragan

"From the beginning, Fort Worth fans had always loved players with some personality. The name of the game was entertainment. Kraft and Pate and the rest weren't the first Cats who had personality. One of the players with an early Fort Worth team [1913] was named John King. He was a left-handed batter who feasted on the pitches of right-handers. But King could not hit a curve ball thrown by a left-hander if he knew ahead of time that it was coming. So anytime he had to step into the batter's box against a southpaw, he would point his bat at the pitcher and snarl, 'Don't throw me a curveball if you want to live.' He meant it. The Fort Worth fans ate it up.

"King was a mean, mean man. One time an opposing infielder, Wally Dashiell, who would be my manager when I played in the minor leagues, pulled the old hidden-ball trick on King. He made the mistake of gloating, 'John, take a look at what I've got!' King screamed, 'You son of a bitch, don't touch me with that ball!' and chased Dashiell clean off the field and under the stands. Dashiell kept yelling over his shoulder to King that he swore he wouldn't tag him, but he couldn't stop running because King kept hollering, 'I'm going to kill you, boy!' I suppose one of the braver umpires eventually had to rule King out for leaving the playing field.

"King eventually didn't play well enough to justify his remaining on the Cats roster. I've been told that his manager just couldn't summon up the courage to tell King he was through. So he got a bright idea. Whenever Fort Worth was on the road, King enjoyed sitting on the front porch of the hotel where the team might be staying. So the manager went to a window a couple of stories over the porch and wrote a note to King telling him he had been released. Then he lowered the note on a string and dangled it in front of his now-former player.

"I'm happy to say King's story ended well. He never did make it to the major leagues, but he went into business around Fort Worth and made a fortune. Probably the people he did business with were afraid not to let him make a big profit on every deal."

The 1920 baseball season was momentous, both nationwide and in Fort Worth. Locally, Atz's Cats, as the newspapers often referred to the team, made a mockery of the Texas League race. The Cats eventually found themselves ahead of second-place Shreveport by 8½ games. Trying to maintain fan interest in cities other than Fort Worth, league officials again split the season so the first- and second-half champions could be matched at season's end for the overall title. They needn't have bothered. Fort Worth won the second half by 12 games. The Cats' season, though, wasn't quite through.

Bobby Bragan:

> "J. Walter Morris and Paul LaGrave talked with Amon Carter, the publisher of the newspaper in Fort Worth. Together, they contacted Bob Allen, whose team from Little Rock had won the Southern Association title, and suggested a post-season series between their respective champions. The Southern Association was supposed to be a better league than the one in Texas. The Cats beat Little Rock four games to two. That made the Cats the champions of the whole South and Southwest, a whole lot of territory. And because of the media interest in baseball that was spreading all across the country, you better believe baseball fans everywhere heard about this super team from Fort Worth."

After the 1919 season, the Boston Red Sox had traded a pitcher and sometime outfielder to the New York Yankees. The Red Sox owner invested heavily in theatrical productions and was short on cash; the Yankees provided the cash and secured the services of Babe Ruth. Ruth became an instant superstar, walloping 54 home runs in his first Yankee season. The biggest papers were in New York and neighboring northeastern cities; soon the news wires were full of baseball stories. This was the beginning of the 1920s and an American sports golden age.

For the first time, professional sports dominated headlines. (Even two or three years earlier, collegiate rowing competitions between schools like Harvard and Yale were considered more important stories than whether the Yankees beat the Red Sox in that day's game.) Baseball's earlier biggest headlines were reserved for the so-called Black Sox scandal in 1919. Eight Chicago players, including all-time great Shoeless Joe Jackson, were banned for life after being accused of conspiring to throw the World Series to the underdog Cincinnati Reds.

Now baseball was what America was talking about. In much of the country, the talk centered around whether the Fort Worth Cats could hold their own against Ruth and the Yankees. More than a few Texas fans were convinced they could.

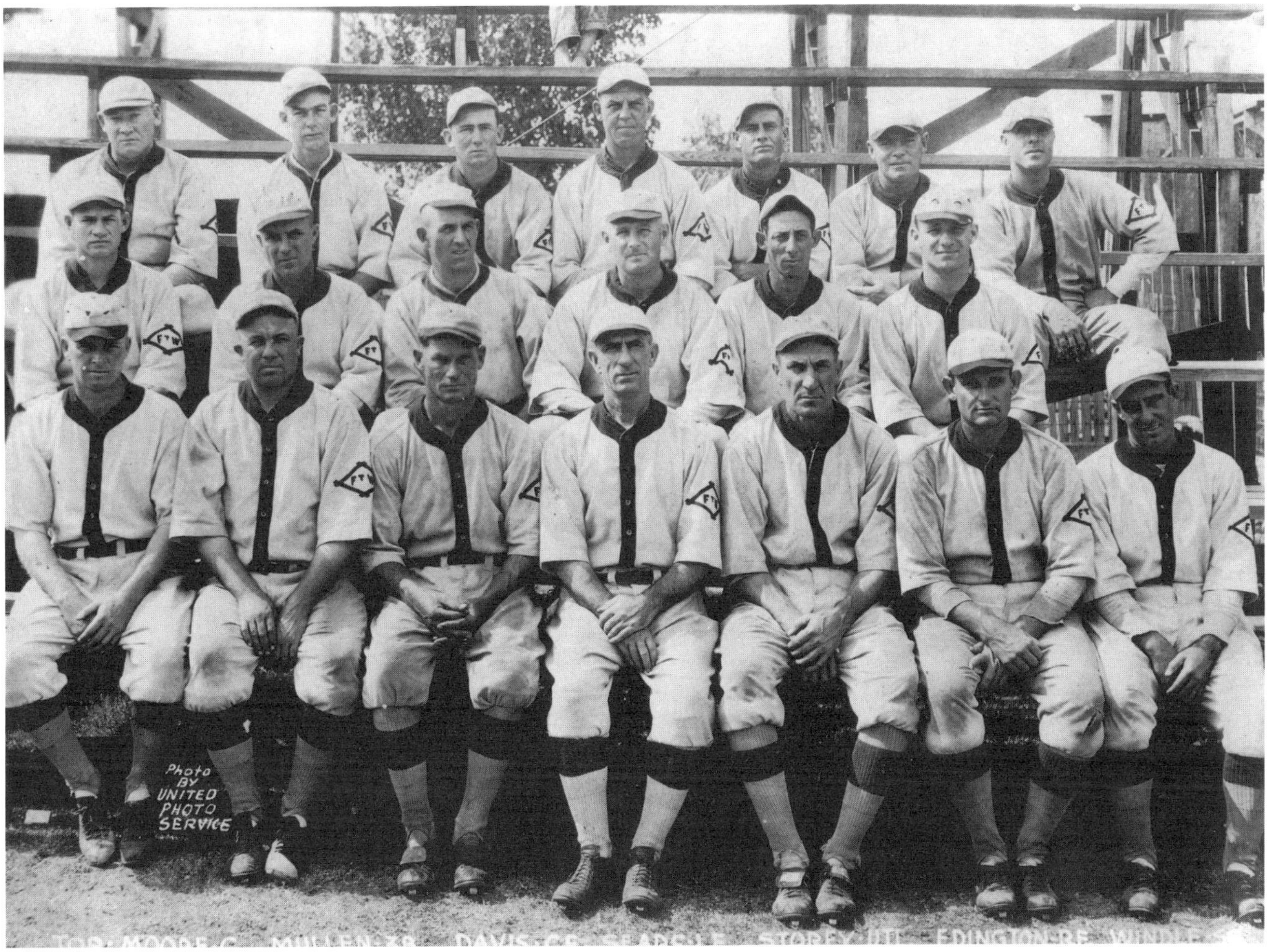

The 1925 Fort Worth Cats—Jake Atz's last championship team (Bobby Bragan Collection).

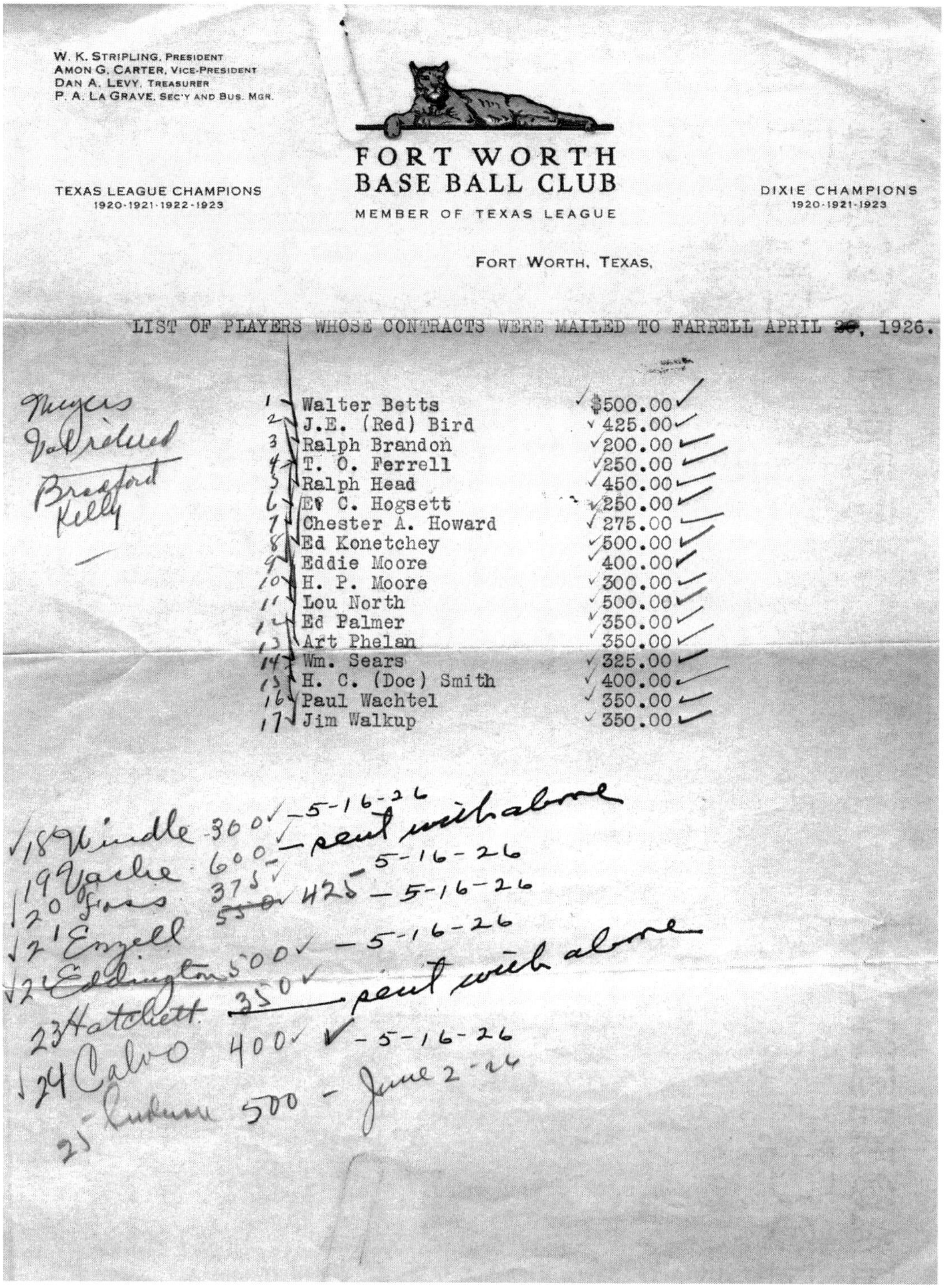

W. K. STRIPLING, PRESIDENT
AMON G. CARTER, VICE-PRESIDENT
DAN A. LEVY, TREASURER
P. A. LA GRAVE, SEC'Y AND BUS. MGR.

FORT WORTH
BASE BALL CLUB
MEMBER OF TEXAS LEAGUE

TEXAS LEAGUE CHAMPIONS
1920-1921-1922-1923

DIXIE CHAMPIONS
1920-1921-1923

FORT WORTH, TEXAS,

LIST OF PLAYERS WHOSE CONTRACTS WERE MAILED TO FARRELL APRIL ~~20~~, 1926.

1	Walter Betts	$500.00
2	J.E. (Red) Bird	425.00
3	Ralph Brandon	200.00
4	T. O. Ferrell	250.00
5	Ralph Head	450.00
6	E? C. Hogsett	250.00
7	Chester A. Howard	275.00
8	Ed Konetchey	500.00
9	Eddie Moore	400.00
10	H. P. Moore	300.00
11	Lou North	500.00
12	Ed Palmer	350.00
13	Art Phelan	350.00
14	Wm. Sears	325.00
15	H. C. (Doc) Smith	400.00
16	Paul Wachtel	350.00
17	Jim Walkup	350.00

Meyers
Vandrelen
~~Bradford~~
Kelly

18 Windle 300 – 5-16-26 – sent with above
19 Yache 600
20 Foss 375 ~~530~~ 425 – 5-16-26
21 Engell – 5-16-26
22 Eddington 500 – 5-16-26
23 Hatchett 350 – sent with above
24 Calvo 400 – 5-16-26
25 Ludmer 500 – June 2-26

Cats letterhead from the office of Paul LaGrave listing player salaries for the 1926 season (Mark Presswood Collection).

Bobby Bragan:

> "Maybe not in every game, of course, but I would not have dismissed Jake Atz's chances in many games against major-league teams. Atz was a fine manager. Don't underestimate what he and the Cats could have done."

Ruth has a special place in Fort Worth baseball lore. When Atz's Cats faced the Yankees in an exhibition game, Fort Worth pitcher Jimmy Walkup struck out the Babe three times in a row. Ruth didn't like it. Afterwards, he told Cats outfielder Ziggy Sears, "I could kick 'em up there harder than that guy throws." Later, Ruth added, "I'm in the big leagues, and he ain't."

Vincent Devaney:

> "You hear the Walkup story all the time, but Ruth got a lot more hits off us than any of us ever struck him out. I pitched against him in an exhibition game, too, though after I left the Cats. The game was somewhere back east. There was a big fence in right field, a high hill behind the fence, and a higher mountain behind the hill. First time up against me, Ruth hit a ball over the fence, over the hill and almost over the mountain. He laughed while he was running around the bases.
>
> "The second time he came up, I did better. He hit a line drive off the first baseman's chest and only got a single. Of course, they had to carry the first baseman off the field."

The 1920 season—Fort Worth's composite record was 108-40—was no aberration. Over the next five Texas League seasons, the Cats won 107, 109, 96, 109 and 103 games. Fort Worth's success was shared by the entire Texas League; the NAPBL promoted it to an "A" league ranking.

In 1921 the Cats were atop the minor-league baseball world. They weren't entirely alone there. In Baltimore, owner/manager Jack Dunn was in the middle of guiding his Orioles to seven consecutive International League pennants. Dunn had previously been best-known for signing Babe Ruth to his first professional contract. Now he proved his talents went beyond recognizing a single great player.

In a sense, Baltimore and Fort Worth complemented each other. Publications like *The Sporting News* covered their seasons in almost as much detail as those of major-league clubs. The two teams would never meet, and perhaps it was just as well. Fans of each were convinced their team would easily defeat the other; if for no other reason, transportation problems kept the match up from taking place.

Some believe the Cats' superlative 107-51 season in 1921 cemented the team's greatness. Two good years in a row was not uncommon among Texas League franchises; this third title proved the Cats were way ahead of the pack. Position by position, they glittered. Possum Moore was still behind the plate; his .298 batting average was third best among the starters. Big Boy Kraft remained at first, and in 1921 he slugged 31 homers, knocked in 141 runs and batted .352. Tex Hoffman held down second, while "Topper" Rigney replaced Bobby Stow at short. Rigney eventually joined the Detroit Tigers. The rest of the everyday lineup found Frank Haley at third, Ziggy Sears, Cecil Coombs and Dugan Phelan in the outfield, and either Joe Pate, Paul Wachtel, Bill Whittaker or Lefty Johns on the mound. Pate pitched 333 innings in 52 games, winning 30 and losing just nine. The Cats' cumulative earned run average was 2.75.

Since the Cats won both halves of the Texas League season, they automatically advanced to the Dixie Series. The Southern Association was willing now to enter into a formal, annual match up with the Texas League champs. Since the Texas League had joined the Southern Association as an "A" league, the series could be billed as a contest between equals. It was that in name only. The Cats blew away Memphis; their fans could and did claim their team was the best among all minor-league squads.

1922 found Will Stripling and Paul LaGrave buying out other partners to take complete financial control of the Cats. It was another walkover season for Fort Worth; the Cats won both halves and were never seriously challenged, even when the Wichita Falls Spudders ran off 24 consecutive victories. It would have been 25, but opponents in that game charged Wichita Falls players with doctoring the baseball and a league investigation confirmed the accusation. It was an odd season for the Spudders. In June, their ballpark caught fire during a game and burned to the ground. Twenty-seven years later, Fort Worth players and fans would know almost the same feeling.

In 1922, Big Boy Kraft won the first of three consecutive league home-run titles. His 131 runs batted in led the league, too. Wachtel's 26 wins were the most of any Texas League pitcher, and Lefty Johns' 21-5 mark was the highest overall winning percentage. Johns also topped the league with a 2.34 earned run average.

Cats' fans were confident heading into the Dixie Series against Southern Association champ Mobile. But Atz's Cats lost, despite the presence during away games of hundreds of screaming Fort Worth fans. Amon Carter had leased a train, dubbed the "Dixie Special," to ferry Cats fans from Texas to Alabama for the games. Cats backers unfortunate enough to be left behind in Fort Worth were able to follow the games on a huge downtown scoreboard. That was also the first season WBAP radio broadcast some Cats games.

In 1923, the Cats did it again. They slipped to 96 wins, but still took the Texas League regular-season title by 13½ games over second-place San Antonio. Atz had his usual core of veteran stars, and New Orleans was no match for Fort Worth in the Dixie Series.

There was no reason for Cats fans to suspect their beloved dynasty was in danger of slipping back to the rest of the Texas League pack. In 1924 Kraft, Pate, Phelan, Moore, Wachtel and the rest were still on the Fort Worth roster.

Bobby Bragan:

> "Big Boy Kraft just went crazy at the plate in '24. He hit 55 home runs, batted around .350 and knocked in 196, still the Texas League record. He was the kind of guy who thrived on attention; the more he got, the more he wanted. He used to tell people that if his name didn't get in the newspaper often enough, he was tempted to punch somebody in the nose just so a reporter would write a story about it.
>
> "Around this time, the Cats were openly hated by other teams in the Texas League. They beat everyone so much, and the Fort Worth players believed it was almost impossible for them to lose. One of the reasons it is so hard for any professional sports team to win its league consistently, besides the problem of keeping a team's players together, is overcoming the focus every opponent has of wanting to beat you more than anyone else. Ballplayers of any era are competitive by nature. The few times Fort Worth would lose each season, you can be certain the players on the teams that beat them celebrated far into the night."

Because of the Cats, the Texas League gained a reputation as one of the best minor leagues anywhere in the country. The league's image was also helped by the success several Texas-born players were achieving in the major leagues, Tris Speaker the best known among them.

In 1924 for the sixth consecutive season the Cats led the Texas League at year's end. In the Dixie League Series—now described in print by *The Sporting News* and other prestigious publications as the "Little World Series"—the Cats crushed Memphis. All was right in the Fort Worth Cats' world until Big Boy Kraft informed Paul LaGrave he was retiring from baseball, effective immediately.

Bobby Bragan:

"At the time he announced his retirement, Clarence Kraft was 37 years old. There was no reason to believe he could not have kept up his impressive production at the plate. But Kraft had other ideas, and it's hard to blame him. He had no intention of leaving Fort Worth; he wanted to use his popularity there to greater financial advantage. So Big Boy purchased a Ford dealership downtown and waited for customers to rush in, all wanting to brag to their friends that they purchased their new cars from the great Big Boy Kraft. It didn't work out quite that way. The dealership became crowded with visitors, but no one wanted to buy a car. Instead, they all wanted to talk baseball with Kraft. Finally, he felt forced to post a notice that no one could come in and discuss baseball without purchasing a car first.

"As with many former Fort Worth players, Kraft's post-baseball life in his adopted hometown was a happy one. Eventually he was elected a county judge, and he served in that office with distinction. And, unlike what many baseball fans in the state predicted, the Cats proved in 1925 they could win even without their most feared slugger."

Mark Presswood:

"Paul LaGrave was up to the challenge of replacing Kraft. He put his nationwide baseball contacts to good use and signed Big Ed Konetchy to take Kraft's place at first base. All Big Ed did in 1925 was hit .345 and lead the Texas League with 41 homers and 166 RBIs. Paul Wachtel won 23 games, the Cats won both halves of the 1925 Texas League season, and they finshed 103-48. Actually, the Cats didn't win the second half of the season. They tied Dallas. Jake Atz challenged Dallas to a best-of-five playoff series. The Cats won the first three games, and then, as Texas League champs for the sixth year in a row, they whipped Atlanta four games to two in the Dixie Series."

Then, gradually, it all fell apart for the Cats.

Besides having Atz as manager, the key to the team's continued success was keeping its best players season after season. Konetchy had been able to step in for Kraft, but in 1926 Joe Pate went on to pitch for Connie Mack and the Philadelphia A's. He pitched well, too, compiling a perfect 9-0 record. Jimmy Walkup, who replaced Pate in the Cats' rotation, won 22, but the consistent level of high play that had characterized Fort Worth was gone. The Cats finished third in the Texas League in 1926. Their 83-73 record left them 6½ games behind league-leading Dallas. No one panicked. Will Stripling still owned the team and Paul LaGrave still ran it. If

1926 hadn't brought with it a seventh consecutive Texas League title, it had included a new Panther Park just a few blocks east of the old one. This park was considered a wonder; it was the first in the league built with steel as well as wood. Despite their heroes' third-place finish, Cats fans kept filling the park, too.

The next two years, 1927 and 1928, were more of the same; the Cats finished fourth and third. One by one, the stalwarts from the glory years dropped off the roster. Atz still managed the club, but Wichita Falls, Dallas and Houston dominated Fort Worth and the rest of the league.

Paul LaGrave died unexpectedly just before the 1929 season. Stripling re-named Panther Park LaGrave Field in his honor and then looked for a buyer for the club. He didn't want to own the Cats if LaGrave wasn't there to run the team for him. Ted Robinson, a businessman who'd previously dabbled in other Texas League franchises, was glad to acquire the famous Cats. On July 1st, the new owner did the unthinkable: He fired Jake Atz and replaced him with Frank Snyder.

Atz wasn't out of a job long. Dallas, now calling its club the Steers (they'd later be named the Rebels, Eagles and Spurs), Fort Worth's arch rival, hired Atz as its manager for the 1930 season. Without his old core of Cats greats, Atz couldn't do much. Dallas finished the year 58-93. Atz would continue to manage minor league clubs through 1941, including one short stint back at the Fort Worth helm in 1933. But the Atz magic was mostly used up; there was only one full-season first-place finish in his future, in 1939 with Henderson of the tiny East Texas League.

With Atz gone and Kraft selling Fords, loyal Cats fans were left to wonder just how good the 1919-1925 Fort Worth teams had really been. Could they have held their own in the major leagues? Even today, it's a matter of unresolvable debate.

Bobby Bragan:

> "Jake Atz was a great manager, just great. He didn't win much after he left Fort Worth, but even the best managers can't win if they don't have the horses. Plenty of fine players were on the Cats' rosters during those great years in the '20s. Pate, you might recall, had a perfect record pitching for Connie Mack in the American League in 1926. Kraft would have been a feared hitter at any level. Had those Cats been magically placed in the American or National League of their era, they might not have knocked off Ruth and the Yankees, but they wouldn't have finished last, either."

Bob Bluthardt:

"Of course, in the minds of their fans the Fort Worth Cats of the '20s were the equivalent of the New York Yankees. The Cats won and they won and they won. There were certainly very successful minor-league teams that, because of sustained success, had a legitimate regional following. Baltimore under Jack Dunn is a good example. But Fort Worth may have represented the largest area of territory of any well-known team, those in the major leagues included. The Cats belonged to Fort Worth and, in a larger sense, to the West and South. They gave people in those regions the chance to look to the northeast and boast, 'We've got something great that you haven't got. They're ours.'

"How good were Jake Atz's Cats, really? Look at how many of his players went on to bigger, better things in professional baseball after they left Fort Worth. A few did. Most didn't. But I would think it is not as important whether the Cats were as good as most major-league teams, but whether the Fort Worth fans believed their team was playing on a major-league level. The Cats served the purpose of their community. They gave their city and their region a reason to feel proud.

"That was the beauty of it, really—the Fort Worth Cats existed in their own little world, and the people of Fort Worth and the Southwest appreciated what they had."

5

Dropping Back to the Pack

Bobby Bragan:

"Today, most people just think of the Great Depression as a few words strung together. But if affected all of our lives back then—it blighted so many good things. Saving every cent possible became standard in Americans' lives, particularly those in rural communities, in southern and western farming communities. I tell a story about my family in those days, and I'm not sure anyone under 50 or so believes it. In the morning my mother would bake biscuits for the family. We would adorn the biscuits with syrup poured from a big gallon can. There were nine of us kids, and the syrup was beloved by all. One morning the freshly baked biscuits were on the table, someone brought over the gallon can and there was a dead mouse floating in the syrup. So we threw out the mouse, but we kept the syrup. You did not waste anything.

"Baseball was still special to most people, but going to games became a luxury. If you barely have enough money to feed your family, you could not spend 50 cents or a dollar on tickets to a game in the Texas League even if Dizzy Dean or Hank Greenberg might be playing—and both did play in the Texas League during the '30s.

"Team owners knew the crisis they were facing. They had to find a way of attracting people to the games who had not attended before. The obvious solution, the one they chose, was playing games at night."

Until 1930, professional games were almost universally played in daylight, though there were a few scattered night games that counted only as exhibitions. Introducing night baseball to regular-season play was seen as a way to attract the so-called "working people" whose full-time jobs during the day prevented them from getting to ballparks before dark. Team owners' philsophy was coldhearted but pragmatic. With the country in the grip of the Great Depression, people who had time during the day to come to games probably had no jobs and couldn't afford tickets. People with jobs could afford them. Most of those people with jobs could only come at night. There had to be night games.

The first regular season night game played between professional baseball teams took place on April 28, 1930, in Independence, Kansas. The first Texas League night game was played in Waco just two months later. The

Katy Park, Waco, home of the first Texas League night game between the Fort Worth Cats and the Waco Navigators (Mark Presswood Collection).

The 1930 Cats—Texas League and Dixie Series champions (Mark Presswood Collection).

Fort Worth Cats lost 13-0 to the hometown Navigators. By 1931, almost half the Texas League games were played at night, except in Beaumont and Wichita Falls. Those two clubs hadn't equipped their parks with lights.

In 1933, Texas League officials came up with another plan to boost late-season attendence. Instead of splitting seasons into two halves, the league adopted the so-called "Shaughnessy Playoff Plan." At year's end, the team in first place took on the team in fourth, while the second- and third-place teams met. The winners of those series were matched for the Texas League championship and the right to represent the league in the Dixie Series. The idea, of course, was to keep fan interest longer; fans of teams battling for fourth place in the eight-team league could believe their hometown club still had a chance to win it all.

And occasionally in the years from the start of the Depression to the Texas League hiatus during World War II, the Fort Worth Cats did win it all. But they didn't do it often. The decade got off to a good start. Wichita Falls won the first half of the 1930 season; the Cats won the second half and won the subsequent playoff against the Spudders to advance to the Dixie Series. Once there, they beat Memphis. Fort Worth fans could be forgiven for believing it was going to be almost like the Atz era again.

Frank Snyder was a colorful manager. His own major-league days had been spent with the New York Giants, and his 1930s Cats featured 20-game winners Dick McCabe and Dick Whitworth. But subsequent seasons weren't kind to Snyder or the Cats. By 1933 Fort Worth was wallowing near the bottom of the league and Snyder was long gone. Disaster struck in 1935—the Cats, at 64-95, finished dead last. Team leadership changed far more often than had been traditional; at one point the Cats ran through seven managers in six seasons, including Jake Atz's brief return to the helm in 1933.

In 1936 the Cats were able to claw their way back over .500, and in 1937 the Cats came under the leadership of longtime Texas League star Homer Peel. Many referred to Peel as "the Ty Cobb of the Texas League"; he'd been a star outfielder for Houston, but he never played better than he did for the Cats in his first year as Fort Worth's manager. Even so, Peel's .370 batting average and 118 runs batted in only propelled his team as far as third place during the regular season. Still, this gave Fort Worth its first chance to participate in the season-ending Shaughnessy play-offs.

The 1930 Dixie Series players—Memphis and Fort Worth (Bobby Bragan Collection).

The Cats met second-place Tulsa in the opening round and won three games to two. This enabled the Cats to move on to Oklahoma City, which had won the regular season by 11½ games. This time, though, Fort Worth triumphed four games to two and went on to the Dixie Series. There the Cats beat Little Rock four games to one, and Fort Worth fans had another Little World Series championship to celebrate.

The Texas League celebrated its 50th anniversary in 1938, but the Cats didn't enjoy themselves much. Fort Worth ended up in eighth place again, winning just 61 games and losing 99. Peel was dismissed. He caught on with Shreveport for the 1940 season and later played with Oklahoma City.

Though the country and region were slowly getting back on better financial footing, league owners decided before the 1939 season to allow radio broadcasts only of away games, reasoning that hometown fans able to listen to their team's games wouldn't have sufficient incentive to get out to the ballpark and buy tickets.

Bob Linton took over as Cats' manager. He built his team around a strong pitching staff, and the Cats squeaked into the Shaughnessy playoffs by finishing fourth, just one game ahead of fifth-place Shreveport. Again, the Cats were at their best in post-season play. Fort Worth defeated

Houston first, then arch-rival Dallas to advance to the Dixie Series, edging Nashville there four games to three.

There were just three more seasons before the Texas League shut down for the duration of World War II. The Cats didn't distinguish themselves in the first two, finishing last in 1940 and fifth in 1941. In 1942, though, Fort Worth fans had another reason to come to LaGrave Field. The team's new manager didn't have the glittering record of Jake Atz, but he still was arguably the best and most famous player ever to come out of Texas.

Bobby Bragan:

"Rogers Hornsby was a baseball legend, and he deserved to be. He was born in Winter, Texas, and as an adult for many years made his home in Fort Worth. In the major leagues Hornsby played for St. Louis, New York, Chicago and Boston, always hitting for power and an incredible average. Three times, he batted over .400. Seven times, he won his league's batting championship. Following his retirement as an active player in 1937, he was eventually elected to the Hall of Fame.

"Late in his big-league career, Hornsby became a player-manager. Except for one early season, those teams he managed were not successful. Returning to Texas, he began managing in the Texas League. In 1942 he was in Fort Worth. If for no other reason, Cats' fans could come to LaGrave Field and know they were seeing one of baseball's all-time greats."

"Hornsby was hard-nosed, a tough man. Some people described him as mean. If he got mad at one of his players, he might urinate on his leg in the shower after the game."

"Hornsby's players complained about that when he managed in the major leagues, too. He brought the custom with him to Fort Worth."

Mark Presswood:

"The men who played for him while he managed the Cats all seemed to have stories about him. One involved why Hornsby got in the habit of never leaving the dugout when he wanted to change pitchers. It seems one night at LaGrave his pitcher was getting hit hard and Hornsby walked to the mound to pull him out of the game. The pitcher swore he could get the next hitter out. Hornsby believed him. Just about the time Hornsby had walked all the way back to the dugout, the batter hit a home run. After that, Hornsby wouldn't take the chance his pitcher might convince him to stay in the game. He'd just sit in the dugout and point his finger at the pitcher. That meant, 'You're coming out now. Get off the mound.'"

Bill Lillard:

"Hornsby favored people who gambled."

William Clark:

"He hated pitchers because he was such a great hitter. I sometimes thought he hated his own pitchers. He had a great pair of eyes. I don't know, but it was rumored he played the horses in each town on our schedule."

Herbert Bain:

"Playing for Rogers Hornsby was the highlight of my career. He was tough but fair. He had the greatest eyes I ever looked into. I met and played with great ballplayers—Gabby Hartnett, Carl Hubbell, Van Lingle Mungo, Mel Ott ... but Rogers Hornsby was the best.

"We were in a tie game in Houston one Sunday. Hornsby (then 46) had to play because our second baseman was hurt. The score was tied 2-2 in the top of the ninth inning. We had men on second and third. First base was open. Hornsby was up. He had struck out twice. Clay Hopper was managing Houston. A lefthander—I don't recall his name—was pitching for Houston. They had a conference on the mound. We all figured they would walk Hornsby to get to Alex Hale, our first baseman who was the only left-handed hitter we had. But instead they chose to pitch to Hornsby, and he hit the first pitch off the top of the scoreboard in left field. We won the game 4-2. After the game Hornsby said, 'They ought to know they can't get me out all the time.'"

Hornsby brought the '42 Cats home in third place, but Shreveport eliminated Fort Worth four games to three in the opening round of the play-offs. The Cats were done for the year, and for three more years after that.

Texas League officials had planned to play a 1943 season, but in February team owners voted 6-2 to suspend play until the war was over. A league office was kept open, however, and officials paid annual dues to the NAPBL to protect their territorial rights.

When the Texas League got back in business for the 1946 season, Rogers Hornsby was gone from the Cats dugout. That wasn't the most significant difference for the Cats and their fans. Thanks to the vision of one man, minor-league baseball had begun a radical change in 1921. A quarter-century later, Branch Rickey turned his attention to Fort Worth, and, because of him, Cats' baseball entered its second great era.

Cats player-manger Homer Peel, pictured during his playing days with the New York Giants (Mark Presswood Collection).

Branch Rickey (Bobby Bragan Collection).

6
Mr. Rickey

Branch Rickey was, at best, a borderline major-league player. His record as a big-league manager wasn't outstanding, either.

The native of Lucasville, Ohio, a catcher and outfielder, played just three seasons and part of a fourth in the majors with the St. Louis Browns in 1905 and 1906, the New York Yankees in 1907 and the Browns again for two at bats in 1914. Rickey couldn't hit a breaking ball, but his baseball brain was formidable. He ended up managing the Browns from 1913 to 1915 and then the St. Louis Cardinals from 1919 to 1925. His teams had a cumulative 597-664 record.

A bad manager and a worse player—yet Branch Rickey is in the Hall of Fame. He earned his way there as a baseball innovator. Abner Doubleday gets credit—perhaps undeserved—for inventing the game, but few realize how much honor Branch Rickey deserves for refining it.

Rickey is best known, of course, for signing Jackie Robinson to a Brooklyn Dodgers contract and, in 1947, breaking baseball's so-called "color barrier." But a Rickey accomplishment of equal baseball weight—if not social impact—was how he completely restructured the entire minor-league system of professional baseball.

Until the late teens, minor-league clubs were independently owned and operated, and players were under contract to team owners. Thanks to NAPBL rules, affiliated minor-league clubs had protected territories and some assurance the players they signed each year couldn't jump to another team for more money.

Club owners made money in two ways, from ticket sales and from selling their best players to other minor-league clubs or, occasionally, to major-league teams. There might even be special understandings between a minor- and major-league club that allowed the big-league team to have first purchase rights for the minor-league team's best player at the conclusion of a season.

But most minor-league players learned the game at the discretion of whatever team owner and manager they played for; some minor-league

Cats players Wyman Honnicutt and Eldon Hill in 1940 (Mark Presswood Collection).

Eddie Snider rounds the bases in 1946 (Fort Worth Star-Telegram *Photograph Collection, Special Collections Division, The University of Texas at Arlington Libraries [hereafter credited as Special Collections, UTA]).*

clubs emphasized teaching and fundamentals, while others simply ran nine players out on the field each day in hopes that enough fans would pay to watch the game. Teams like the Fort Worth Cats and Baltimore Orioles enjoyed long-term success because their owners tried to retain a core of good players from season to season. Still, many minor leaguers played for a different club each season, and the ultimate goal of players was usually to get a chance in the majors.

In 1919, Branch Rickey was both manager and general manager of the St. Louis Cardinals. He had a different vision for the minor leagues; to Rickey, a major-league club should affiliate itself directly with a number of different minor-league squads and use those teams as teaching and development stops for players who would gradually work their way from Class-D ball to the majors. There would be continuity of instruction from one minor-league level to the next; the major-league team's front office would even become actively involved in choosing the managers of their affiliates.

Rickey put his plan into practice. In 1919, the Cardinals sold off their old ballpark, Robinson Field, and used part of the money from the sale to purchase an 18-percent interest in the Houston Buffs of the Texas League. Rickey kept the deal quiet. Though he had full ownership of Houston by 1925, it wasn't common knowledge among fans. Then Rickey went on to acquire bits and pieces of other minor-league clubs at every level from D to Triple-A; eventually he and the Cardinals controlled 32 teams and more than 600 minor-league players.

As a result, St. Louis didn't have to comb every team in every minor league for prospects. It signed the best it could find and assigned them to one of its own farm teams. There, each player's progress could be carefully monitored. And, by the early 1940s, the St. Louis Cardinals had become a National League powerhouse, though Rickey was smart enough to let other people serve as the Cardinals' manager.

Bobby Bragan:

> "Branch Rickey was a big believer in tryout camps, first with the Cardinals and later with the Dodgers. He would let hundreds of players show his scouts what they could do. His were the first tryout camps to include races, tests of running speed. Speed was an asset in an athlete Mr. Rickey greatly admired. He said it was something that could not be learned; either a man could run fast, or he couldn't. He might have his tryout camps begin by having everybody race a few hundred yards, and he would thank those who finished in the bottom half and dismiss them from

the camp. True, he would lose out occasionally on the heavy-legged players who might still be awesome hitters, but he usually ended up with the best athletes."

The "Rickey system" spread. The Detroit Tigers became the second club to develop their own extensive farm system of minor-league teams, and soon every organization had agreements with specific minor-league clubs. The emphasis became teaching players as much as fan entertainment. The fans won, anyway: as players gained a better grasp of baseball fundamentals, the quality of minor-league play across the country improved dramatically.

Joe DiMaggio:

"In 1934, the San Francisco Seals of the Pacific Coast League sold my contract to the New York Yankees. But implicit in this agreement was that I would remain with the Seals for the 1935 season. Lefty O'Doul, the San Francisco manager, had agreed to help alter my batting style to fit Yankee Stadium. I was, at that time, a spray hitter in the sense I hit the ball to all parts of the park. But to succeed as a power hitter in Yankee Stadium, it was necessary to pull the ball down the relatively short foul lines. O'Doul worked with me extensively on this during 1935, and in 1936 I was ready to join the Yankees."

Bobby Bragan:

"The job of a minor-league manager changed. In the major leagues, the manager's job was to win at all costs, every game. The minor-league manager now had to teach first and win second, but the best teachers also won the most, so it evened out.

"If you look at the Houston Buffs teams in the 1920s, you see what Mr. Rickey was working towards. Dizzy Dean, one of the greatest pitchers of all time, put in some learning time in Houston. When he was ready, the Cardinals moved him on up. The Houston stop gave him seasoning. I'm sure his arm was already great when the Cardinals signed him, but the best pitchers have to do more than throw the ball hard.

"I'm happy to say I had the chance to know Mr. Rickey well. I played for the Brooklyn Dodgers when he ran that team. I worked for him as a manager in Fort Worth and later for the Hollywood Stars of the Pacific Coast League. I thank God, and the Fort Worth Cats players and fans ought to thank God, that Branch Rickey eventually decided he wanted a minor-league club in Fort Worth."

Mark Presswood:

"The way Branch Rickey learned about Fort Worth was probably like this: When he ran the Cardinals, Rogers Hornsby was his best player, and Hornsby made his off-season home in Fort Worth. Rickey had to come to Fort Worth to negotiate contracts with Hornsby. I'm sure he looked around the city and liked it."

Bobby Gorbould and Duke Snider in 1946 (Special Collections, UTA).

Rogers Hornsby (back row, center) and the 1942 Cats (Mark Presswood Collection, Courtesy of Scott Hanzelka).

Rickey's minor-league plan wasn't entirely without opposition. Judge Kenesaw Mountain Landis, commissioner of baseball in an era when the commissioner told major-league team owners what he would and would not allow them to do, decided the Cardinals and Tigers were corrupting the spirit of the minor leagues, which Landis believed required minor-league teams to have local ownership and control. An agreement between the St. Louis Browns and the minor-league Milwaukee Brewers was taken to court in 1931, but the court upheld the Browns-Brewers relationship. But in March 1938 and again in January 1940, Landis simply acted on his own; about 120 minor-league players, including 91 of the Cardinals players, were declared free agents by the commissioner. Rickey simply went on acquiring teams and players as he chose.

Eventually, Rickey and the Cardinals parted ways. Nicknamed "The Mahatma," Rickey was welcomed by the ownership of the Brooklyn Dodgers and encouraged to develop an extensive minor-league farm system for the organization. There were plenty of available minor-league clubs. According to writer David Pietrusza in *Minor Miracles*, his excellent study of minor-league history, by 1940 there were 44 minor leagues and 310 minor-league teams in operation. In 1949 minor-league baseball in America hit the high-water mark, with 59 leagues, 448 teams and 9,000 players.

Branch Rickey had long admired the Texas League, and the Fort Worth Cats as yet had no formal affiliation with a major-league team. Rickey set out to change that.

There was time for negotiation, since the Texas League was on hiatus for World War II. But on August 27, 1946, NAPBL president W. G. Branham announced that the Brooklyn Dodgers had purchased the Fort Worth Cats. John L. Reeves, Branham added, would serve as the Cats' president.

Mark Presswood:

"John Reeves had been a secretary and business manager for the Cats in the early '40s. Certainly Branch Rickey was aware of him then, because the first announcement made after word of the sale got out was that Brooklyn was making John Reeves president of the Fort Worth club.

"With their purchase by the Dodgers, the Cats were about to enter what was clearly the second great era of the team. It ought to be noted that both times, during the Atz years and what is usually called the Bragan era, the team had especially strong front-office management.

"And this time around it didn't hurt that Branch Rickey liked Fort Worth enough to send the Cats lots of good players."

Bill Eberle, Cats business manager, John Reeves and Bragan (Bobby Bragan Collection).

Bragan blocks home in an exhibition game against the Brooklyn Dodgers. The base runner is Pee Wee Reese (Bobby Bragan Collection).

The grand opening of Cats' coach Tommy Tatum's service station in 1951 (Bobby Bragan Collection).

7

The Bragan Era

The Bobby Bragan era in Fort Worth baseball began without Bobby Bragan. He was still an active major-league player, catching occasional games for the Brooklyn Dodgers. Bragan's distinct lack of speed—Stan Musial once called him "the slowest man I ever saw play in the majors" —and problems hitting curveballs meant his Dodger days were numbered, but neither he nor the Cats yet realized their paths would cross in another two seasons.

Meanwhile, the Cats and the rest of the Texas League resumed operations. Both the team and league were greatly changed from 1942. It was still an eight-team league; besides the Cats, there were franchises from Dallas, San Antonio, Tulsa, Beaumont, Houston, Shreveport and Oklahoma City. The Texas League classification, though, had been upgraded to Double-A. In theory, this still placed it a rung below Triple-A, the minor-league level at which players were supposed to receive their last instruction before reaching the majors. In practice, major-league teams often promoted players straight from Double-A.

Post-season play-offs for the year's top four teams still existed but were now known collectively as "The Texas League Playoff Plan." Because the team that led the league at the conclusion of the regular season often failed to win the play-offs and advance to the Dixie Series, it was also determined by Texas League owners that each season's first-place club would be presented with the Jake Atz Trophy.

The Brooklyn front office stocked the Cats with some of the finest young players in the Dodger organization. Cats manager Ray Hayworth enjoyed the services of several future major leaguers, including shortstop Johnny Welaj, pitchers Johnny Van Cuyk and Eddie Chandler and a young outfielder named Edwin Snider, who baseball fans would soon call "Duke."

Fort Worth fans had to adjust to a new system of player movement on the Cats' roster. Now the best players in any given season were likely to

Bragan with his 1950 infield: Don Hoak, third base; Russ Rose, shortstop; Joe Torpey second base; Dee Fondy, first base (Bobby Bragan Collection).

Jimmy and Bobby Bragan in 1951 (Bobby Bragan Collection).

be taken away from the team without notice, promoted to Triple-A Montreal or even to Brooklyn and the National League. There was, at least, the consolation of radio. The Yankees, Cardinals and Dodgers had all developed extensive radio networks carrying their game broadcasts around the country. Fort Worth fans could tune in to Brooklyn games and hear how some of their favorite ex-Cats were doing.

The Cats' players themselves found there were distinct advantages about playing for a minor-league team owned by a major-league club. Brooklyn farmhands enjoyed a special benefit—the Dodger spring training camp in Vero Beach, Florida, offered young players an unprecedented opportunity to play alongside experienced major leaguers.

Dick Williams:

"At Vero Beach we lived in some old Navy barracks and roomed four to a room, sleeping on double beds. There were five playing fields and lots of extra areas to practice sliding, bunting, everything. It was the only minor-league camp where kids from Class D teams were right there with the big-league stars. Pee Wee Reese, later Jackie Robinson, they'd be right there with the young kids, and you know their good work habits made a great impression. You'd see these famous players hustling and think, 'Hey, I better work that hard, too.'

"From the major leagues to Class D, the Dodgers wanted—which is to say, Branch Rickey wanted—every player to be taught to do the same things the same way. It wasn't enough, with the Dodgers, for guys to be good athletes. They also had to be smart athletes. We would get tested on basic baseball rules. It was never assumed that you already knew something. I learned so much from listening. Like a lot of other guys who played for the Dodgers or in the Dodger system, when I became a manager years later I used the same things I'd been taught by Rickey and his people 20, 30 years earlier. I'll give you an example: In 1967 I got my first major league managing job with the Boston Red Sox. On the first day of spring training I gave my so-called major-league players a simple test on the rules. One thing I asked was, 'What is the double line that runs partway between home plate and first base?' See, it's the designated area base runners have to stay in. Not complicated, right? But 90 percent of these big-shot Boston Red Sox didn't even know that basic thing. So I did what Mr. Rickey would have wanted his managers to do. I spent the first two days of spring training doing nothing but going over the basic baseball rules until every player had learned them. You might remember, this Red Sox team finished ninth in the league in '66, and my first year in '67 we got all the way to the World Series and gave the Cardinals a hell of a fight before we lost the seventh game. You think the Red Sox players finally knowing the rules didn't help at least a little? And it's the little things that win you ball games. The Dodgers taught us that."

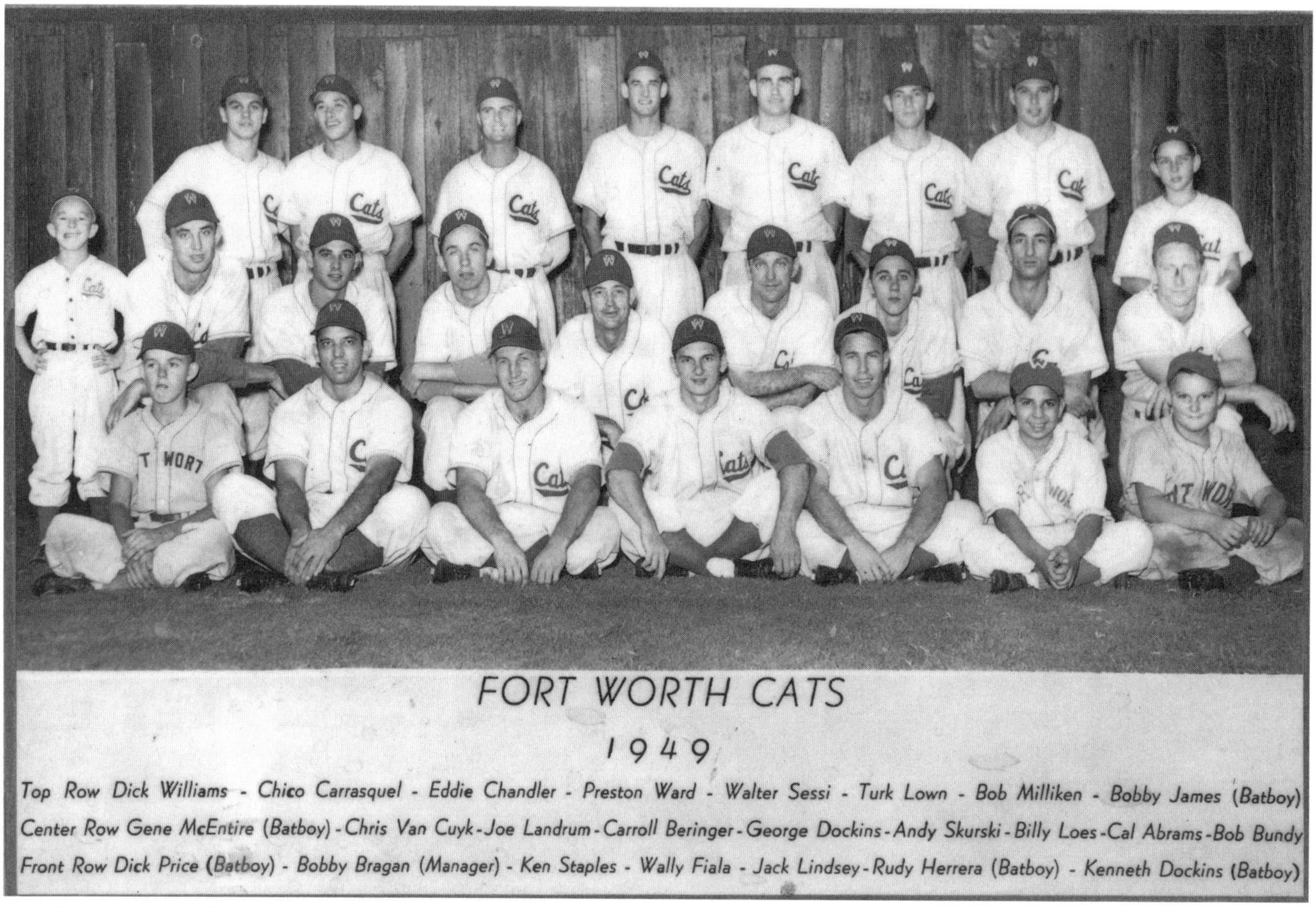

The 1949 Cats (Bobby Bragan Collection).

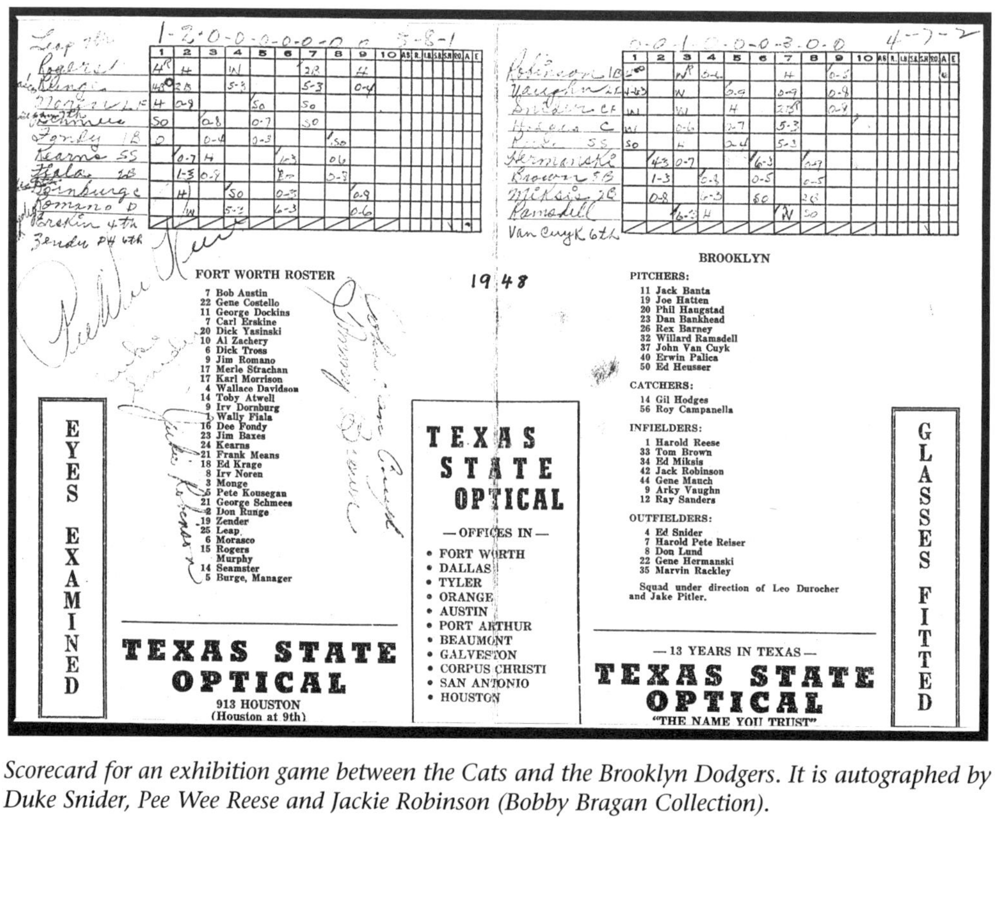

Scorecard for an exhibition game between the Cats and the Brooklyn Dodgers. It is autographed by Duke Snider, Pee Wee Reese and Jackie Robinson (Bobby Bragan Collection).

When the Cats got back to Fort Worth to play their first regular season Texas League games, they played on one of the most attractive, unique home fields in minor-league baseball.

Bobby Bragan:

"LaGrave Field was the envy of most other professional baseball teams, including many in the major leagues. It was the only park whose infield was black dirt. Fuller's Earth, it was called. It was smooth and allowed fair hops on ground balls. There was also a layer of pecan shells underneath. The nearby Ellis Pecan Company ground up shells to a fine powder. That layer absorbed any extra moisture. The area around home plate and the pitcher's mound were red clay. The infield and outfield grass was kept close clipped and green. Mr. Reeves continued the LaGrave tradition of clean bathrooms, very important if you wanted families to come out to support the team. Parking was adequate. There was good public transportation to and from the ballpark. It was an idyllic setting for baseball."

Players, in turn, always gave maximum effort on the field. They were constantly aware that, in an era of expanded farm systems, there were always many other players trying to win the same major-league jobs.

Joe Macko:

"You always knew you were competing daily against the guys who played your position for all the other minor-league teams affiliated with your major-league club. If the Dodgers had 30 farm teams and you played third base, then you knew there were 29 other third basemen with the same goal you had—replacing the guy who was currently playing third base for Brooklyn. You could never completely relax.

"Injuries were ignored. If you got hurt, it had to be damn near fatal to keep you from playing. You expected your regular paycheck, and the bosses expected you to play. So if you broke a finger, you taped it and played. If you look at the hands of lots of guys who played back then, you'll see they have fingers sticking out in every direction. That's because you'd often get bad hops on ground balls—some of the infields in the Texas League, hell, any minor league, were more rocks than dirt—and you'd snap a finger. But you'd keep on playing and eventually the bone would heal strangely."

Dick Williams:

"Hell, yes, we played when we were hurt! The idea was, if you were well enough to get to the park and put your uniform on, you were well enough to play. Later on when Bragan was manager, he also scared the hell out of us. His voice when he yelled had great healing powers. Alex Thomas was the Cats' trainer. He used to make his own rubbing linament. It burned like hell, but it helped. It had a garlic smell to it and also urine. Nobody ever really wanted to know what he put in it."

Unmarried Cats players—and most were—couldn't afford to live in hotels. Instead, the club would refer them to families who had spare bedrooms.

Joe Macko:

> "Boarding with a family would cost about $5 a week, and for that they'd also feed you. More than feed you. When players stayed with families, it was like they were adopted. It was like having a second family and it was especially a comfort for the very youngest guys who hadn't been away from their real families for all that long. You've got to understand, Fort Worth fans loved their Cats."

In 1946, the Cats gave their fans good reason to feel that way. Hayworth led his Dodger farmhands to a 101-53 record and first place in the regular Texas League season. He did it by emphasizing pitching and defense. Eddie Chandler won 20 games, Johnny Van Cuyk 18 and Willard Ramsdell 17, but no Cats hitter managed more than five home runs. First baseman Lou Ruchser's 57 RBIs led the club. One of the Fort Worth hitters to crack five homers was Duke Snider, who didn't stay long with the team. Snider always credited his rapid rise to the majors from the Cats to Branch Rickey's presence at LaGrave Field during one 1946 contest. Snider, who only hit .250 in 232 at-bats, picked a good night to clout a monster home run off the right-field clock tower. Impressed by the kid's power, Rickey soon moved him up to the Dodgers. The Dodger management learned that players promoted from Fort Worth were the kind of athletes Brooklyn wanted on its major-league roster—and not just because of playing ability.

Leo Durocher:

> "Fort Worth players had vinegar. I mean, if we got into a fight, guys from Fort Worth would jump in the middle of it."

Dick Williams:

> "I guess we all did like to rough it up. Except Don Hoak. Hoak started lots of fights he couldn't finish."

The Cats' near-perfect 1946 season, though, had an imperfect ending. Fort Worth easily beat Tulsa 3-1 in the re-named "Texas League Playoff," but arch rival Dallas whipped the Cats in the second round and then swept the Dixie Series from Atlanta.

John Reeves and Bobby Bragan are interviewed on WBAP-TV. Team comptroller Wallace Jay is also present. In 1949 WBAP was the first station to televise Cats games (Bobby Bragan Collection).

Beaumont manager Rogers Hornsby and Bobby Bragan, 1950 (Bobby Bragan Collection).

Bragan and Cats players at the Dodger spring training facility in Vero Beach, Florida. The Dodger plane is in the background (Bobby Bragan Collection).

Cats third baseman Bob Bundy avoids a tag at home plate (Mark Presswood Collection).

There was never any doubt in players' minds regarding the team the Cats wanted most to beat.

Mike Napoli:

"When I first arrived at LaGrave Field, I got called in to meet with the team brass. First question they asked me was, 'Do you know why you're here, Michael?' I said, 'Why?' They said, 'You're supposed to help us beat Dallas more times than Dallas beats us.'"

Jack Lindsey:

"The Dallas rivalry was intense. I remember one year Rex Barney from our team had been placed on the disabled list, and for a game between us and Dallas he sat right behind home plate. The Dallas catcher was giving the signs too low between his legs, and Rex could see them. So he would relay those signs to our first-base coach, and the coach would relay them to us when we stood in the batter's box. I remember the Dallas pitcher throwing me a beautiful curve ball that I lined into left center because I knew it was coming. When I got to first base, he had a look on his face like, 'How did you hit that?'"

In 1947, Les Burge took over as Cats' manager. Burge was a player-manager who started for his club at first base. As was the custom under major-league stewardship, the Fort Worth roster was almost completely different from 1946. Willard Ramsdell was back, and Eddie Chandler would play part of the season in a Cats' uniform. But Fort Worth fans soon fell in love with infielder Wally Fiala, who spent several seasons on the roster, and outfielder Irv Noren, who went on to the major leagues after playing two seasons for Fort Worth.

Thanks to John Reeves' insistence on a clean ballpark and gentlemanly behavior from his players, more men began bringing their wives and daughters to Cats games.

Ann King Patrick and Jan King Rhinefort:

"Dad was a baseball nut. He played semi-pro ball and for Rogers Hornsby's barnstorming teams. He worked at Convair and would take us to LaGrave Field on Sunday afternoons. We got to see Dwain Sloat pitch a no-hitter on August 3, 1947. We really remember that one.

"Dad taught us to keep score and tally stats. We would get an old grocery sack, draw lines on it like a scorecard and keep score at home if we were listening to the Cats' games on radio. When we went to the games, Dad would drive us in an old brown Plymouth. We would sit high in the grandstand behind the Cats' third-base dugout.

> "Pop Pulliam of Pulliam Pools would bring a monkey to the games and entertain kids with the monkey and by tying up balloons to look like animals. There was a peanut vendor who would yell, 'PEE-NER-ITS!' There were also a lot of cigars at LaGrave Field. We would smell cigars later in life and remember being in the ballpark."

The Cats had a good year in 1947, but their 95-58 record was a half-game behind the pennant-winning Houston Buffs. Houston's manager was Johnny Keane, who would later lead the St. Louis Cardinals to a World Series win in 1964 over the New York Yankees. Fort Worth lost to Dallas in the first round of the post-season play-offs, and Houston went on to win the Dixie Series against Mobile, another Dodger Double-A club.

The next year, 1948, proved especially memorable for the Cats: Bobby Bragan arrived.

Burge began the year as Fort Worth's manager. He had a talented team; besides holdovers Noren, Fiala and Chandler, Brooklyn added future major leaguers Dee Fondy and (in mid-season) Dick Williams to the Cats' roster. Best of all, Rickey sent Brooklyn's most prodigious young pitching talent, Carl Erskine, for seasoning on the LaGrave Field mound. Yet, the Cats plodded through the first portion of the season. Some believe John Reeves lost patience with Burge; others contend Rickey and the Dodger front office decided the manager had to go.

Jack Lindsey:

> "Les Burge had everyone on edge. If you made a mistake, you were sitting on the bench quickly. After a losing streak, they decided to replace him."

Mark Presswood:

> "There was some conflict between John Reeves and Les Burge. They didn't get along. A losing streak gave Reeves the opportunity to let Burge go. Les was supposed to be very arrogant. He didn't want any advice on how to run his team."

Bobby Bragan:

> "Mr. Rickey was dissatisfied with the Cats' 1948 performance. He dispatched his right-hand man, Burt Shotton, to Fort Worth and asked him to report on the situation there. Shotton discovered Les Burge did not call for morning workouts before night games. It gave the impression he wasn't concerned enough to teach the fundamentals sufficiently. So Shotton told Mr. Rickey, 'I'm going to recommend a change in managers, and the man I'd recommend is in your bullpen.' You see, I spent most of the 1948 season warming up pitchers for Brooklyn.

Bat boys, 1948 (Bobby Bragan Collection).

Outfielder Irv Noren, the Cat's first Texas League Most Valuable Player, 1948 (Mark Presswood Collection).

LaGrave Field after the May 1949 fire and flood (Mark Presswood Collection).

May 15, 1949—Fort Worth takes on San Antonio in fire-damaged LaGrave Field (Bobby Bragan Collection).

John Reeves, Cats president, surveys the fire damage, 1949 (Mark Presswood Collection).

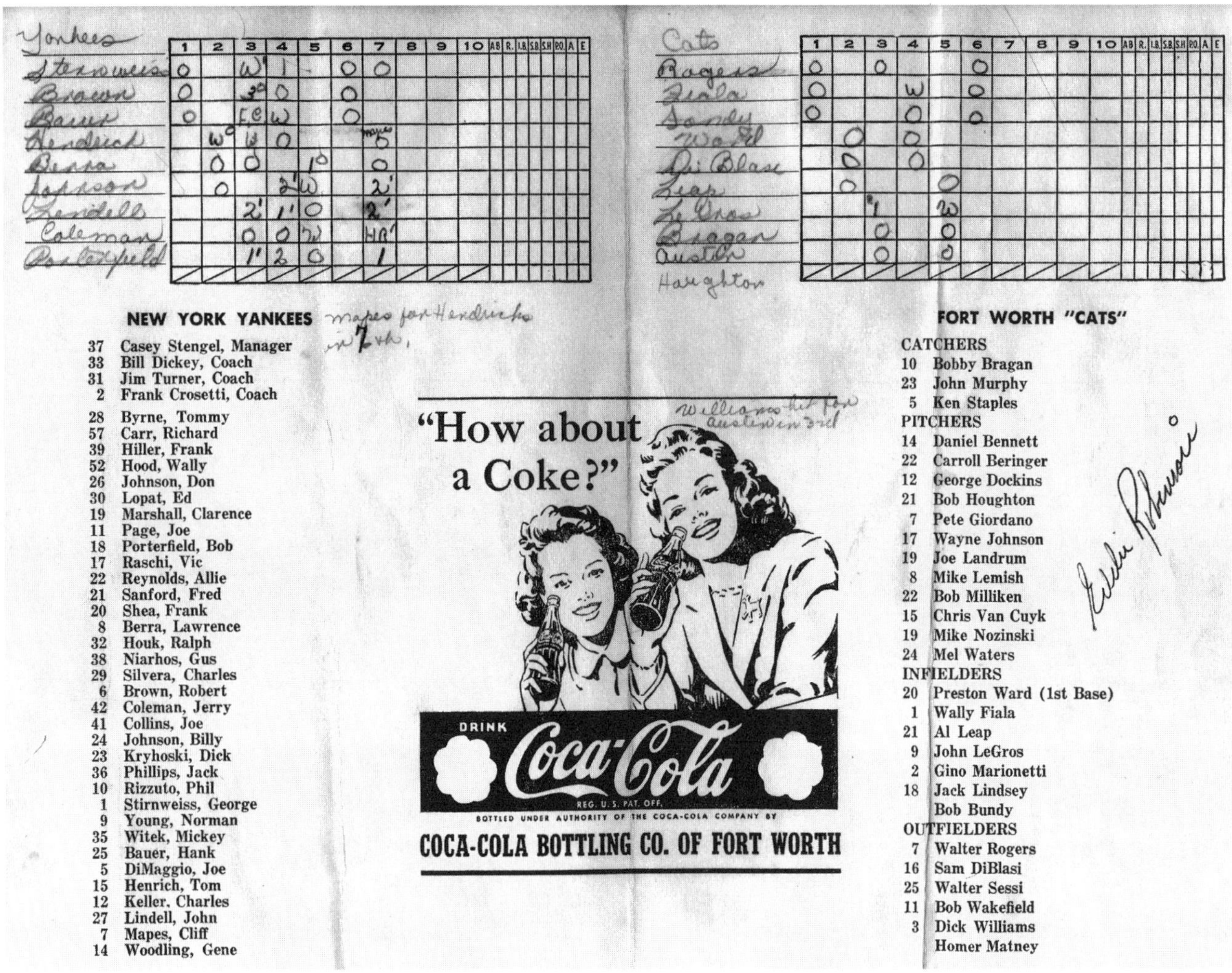

NEW YORK YANKEES

37 Casey Stengel, Manager
33 Bill Dickey, Coach
31 Jim Turner, Coach
2 Frank Crosetti, Coach
28 Byrne, Tommy
57 Carr, Richard
39 Hiller, Frank
52 Hood, Wally
26 Johnson, Don
30 Lopat, Ed
19 Marshall, Clarence
11 Page, Joe
18 Porterfield, Bob
17 Raschi, Vic
22 Reynolds, Allie
21 Sanford, Fred
20 Shea, Frank
8 Berra, Lawrence
32 Houk, Ralph
38 Niarhos, Gus
29 Silvera, Charles
6 Brown, Robert
42 Coleman, Jerry
41 Collins, Joe
24 Johnson, Billy
23 Kryhoski, Dick
36 Phillips, Jack
10 Rizzuto, Phil
1 Stirnweiss, George
9 Young, Norman
35 Witek, Mickey
25 Bauer, Hank
5 DiMaggio, Joe
15 Henrich, Tom
12 Keller, Charles
27 Lindell, John
7 Mapes, Cliff
14 Woodling, Gene

"How about a Coke?"

DRINK Coca-Cola

REG. U. S. PAT. OFF.

BOTTLED UNDER AUTHORITY OF THE COCA-COLA COMPANY BY

COCA-COLA BOTTLING CO. OF FORT WORTH

FORT WORTH "CATS"

CATCHERS
10 Bobby Bragan
23 John Murphy
5 Ken Staples

PITCHERS
14 Daniel Bennett
22 Carroll Beringer
12 George Dockins
21 Bob Houghton
7 Pete Giordano
17 Wayne Johnson
19 Joe Landrum
8 Mike Lemish
22 Bob Milliken
15 Chris Van Cuyk
19 Mike Nozinski
24 Mel Waters

INFIELDERS
20 Preston Ward (1st Base)
1 Wally Fiala
21 Al Leap
9 John LeGros
2 Gino Marionetti
18 Jack Lindsey
Bob Bundy

OUTFIELDERS
7 Walter Rogers
16 Sam DiBlasi
25 Walter Sessi
11 Bob Wakefield
3 Dick Williams
Homer Matney

Scorecard of an exhibition game between the Fort Worth Cats and the New York Yankees on April 12, 1949. Yankee Bob Porterfield pitched an eight-inning no-hitter (Mark Presswood Collection).

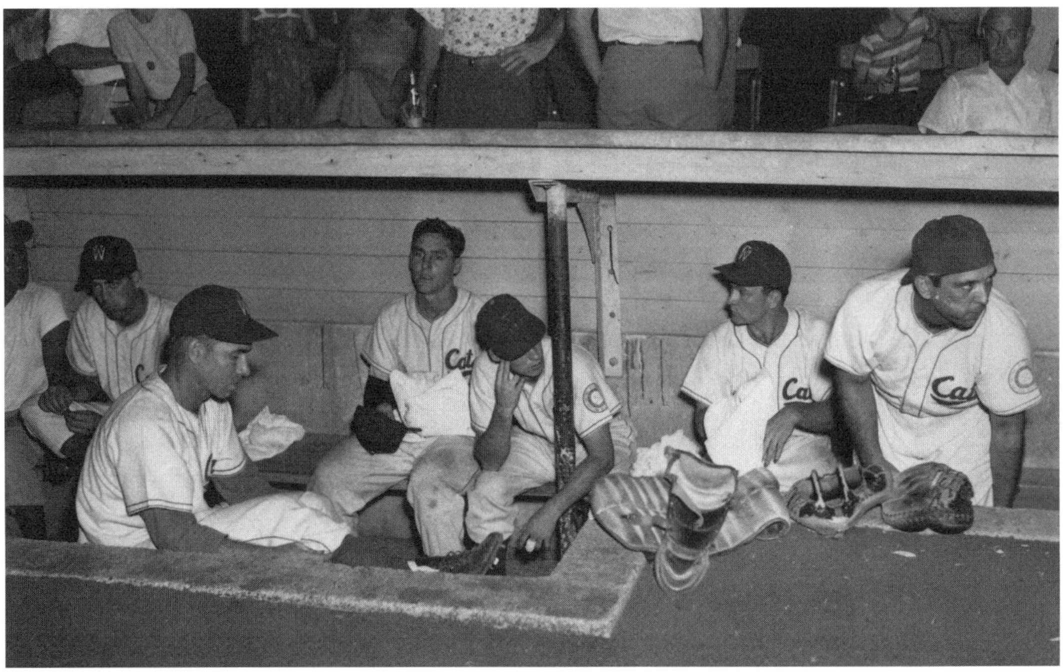

Inside the dugout, 1951 (Bobby Bragan Collection).

"I'd known for some time I'd gone as far as I could as a major-league player. I'd been a shortstop and catcher with the Phillies and Dodgers since 1940. I was slow; I couldn't hit the curve ball. But I knew the game. Now, in 1947 Brooklyn brought Jackie Robinson to the big leagues, and that had been an important time for me. I was from Alabama. I had the prejudices of my home region. But being around Jackie taught me a lot about human beings being equal, and I gradually was able to put aside my prejudice. The Dodgers had another black player in the minors, a catcher named Roy Campanella. He had been a great star in the Negro League before signing with the Dodgers, who sent him to St. Paul to integrate the minor league there. Now, in 1948, Campanella was ready for the major leagues, and I was the Dodger's last-string catcher. Sending me to Fort Worth to manage the Cats would also open up a spot on the Brooklyn roster for Campanella. I always say my greatest contribution to the Dodgers was going away so Campanella could come play for them.

"Mr. Rickey told me it would take a few days for me to clear major-league waivers, but that I would be the next manager of the Fort Worth Cats. It was a tremendous opportunity. Managers moved through a farm system just like players did. Starting at Double-A meant I was, perhaps, second in line to manage the Dodgers after the fellow managing Montreal at Triple-A and Leo Durocher, who was still the Brooklyn manager when I went to Fort Worth."

For the eight-day interim between Burge and Bragan, Reeves asked veteran pitcher George Dockins to run the team. Dockins did a better job than anticipated; the Cats went 9-0 for him. When Bragan finally arrived, joining the Cats before a doubleheader with Tulsa, he asked plaintively, "If they never lose, why are they bringing me in?"

At the ballpark that evening, Bragan met with his new team. He told Fort Worth players he wouldn't have many rules, but he expected his club to follow them. They'd report on time for games, obey curfew, and never stay out later than two hours after night games. The Cats responded by winning the first game of the doubleheader, but they lost the second. They didn't lose many for the rest of the 1948 regular season, finishing a game-and-a-half ahead of second-place Tulsa.

Bobby Bragan:

"My family and I fell in love with Fort Worth. When I took over the Cats, we moved to town to stay. Mr. Rickey always had a story he liked to tell about a man who had been named manager of a minor-league team. When he arrived in this town, he asked someone what sort of place it was. The gist of the story was that a new manager should adapt himself to the town, not expect the town to change to suit him. As it happened, Fort Worth suited the Bragans perfectly.

"I very much enjoyed working with John Reeves. He was a real gentleman. So much so that when I left Fort Worth and the Cats years later, I did so in protest of Mr. Reeves being fired. But that was far in the future.

"The team I inherited from Les Burge was an impressive one. Erskine, of course, was destined to be a major-league star. Though they weren't as well-known, outfielder Irv Noren and first baseman Dee Fondy became solid major leaguers, too. It was a well-balanced team with the emphasis on pitching and defense. I think Noren was our only hitter to hit double figures in home runs. Dick Williams joined the team right after I did, and that young player made a significant contribution to the team, more so in 1949 and 1950 than he did for the remainder of 1948."

Dick Williams:

"I was afraid of Bobby Bragan. He was a great teacher but, boy, if he got mad at you, his words could blister your skin. But he was a great teacher; that was what he thought a minor-league manager should be. He taught you how to act on the field and off it, too. Right away when he got there he started this tradition—if any of his players would go to church with him on Sunday, he'd buy them breakfast. We were kids without much money—I think Bobby knew we were coming for the food as well as the religion. Four or five of us would always go. I think, though, he made some deal with the restaurant and never really had to pay."

Mark Presswood:

"Bobby Bragan wasn't perfect. Most of his former players I've talked to say his effect on their careers was positive, but he did make some people mad. He could be very sarcastic. But no manager is loved by all his players. It doesn't work that way. Casey Stengel used to say that on any of his ball clubs he had five players who loved him, five who hated him and he tried to make sure the other 15 hung out with the five who loved him.

"Carl Erskine tells this story about Bragan. Carl had pitched a game against Dallas and won it. The next night he's sitting on the bench watching the game, eating peanuts and sort of relaxing. The game is tied, and in the ninth Bobby gets up to bat and walks. Bobby was maybe the slowest runner in baseball history, so he calls for Erskine to come in and run for him. Erskine goes out, trying to brush all the peanut shells off his jersey before Bobby sees them. Bragan takes the first-base coach's place and tells Erskine right away, 'Watch this pitcher, because he's got a great pickoff move.' And just as he's saying it, the Dallas pitcher picks Erskine off first. Erskine swears Bobby wouldn't talk to him for three weeks."

Dick Williams:

"Bobby's wife, Gwenn, used to come with us on some road trips. We would be given these box lunches to eat on the way, nothing fancy—maybe a sandwich and an apple. Well, a couple of us started tossing apples around and one I threw almost hit Gwenn Bragan. Bobby put my ass on the bench that night. I asked if it was because I'd nearly hit his wife, and he said it was because I needed to learn it was wrong to throw food."

Carroll Beringer:

"The way I heard the story, Dick Williams threw an orange, and it went between Bobby's legs around his knees. So he benched Williams that night and told him, 'If you'd thrown that thing six inches higher, you'd be back playing in Class D!'"

The Cats hosted the 1948 Texas League All-Star Game at LaGrave Field. It remains a special memory for two of their fans.

Ann King Patrick and Jan King Rhinefort:

"One of our saddest moments is also why we still love baseball so much. Dad had gotten tickets to the 1948 All-Star game in Fort Worth, but he had a stroke and died two days before the game. He was buried on All-Star game day. Right after the stroke he couldn't speak very well, but Mom remembers him telling her she had to make sure we were taken to the game."

After finishing first in the regular season, the Cats easily won the league play-offs. Fort Worth beat Shreveport 4-2 in the first round and qualified for the Dixie Series by eliminating Tulsa four games to three. All four Fort Worth wins were shutouts.

The Dixie Series had a sadder ending. Physically battered after the play-offs—shortstop Jack Lindsey was hurt against Shreveport, and Bragan was injured against Tulsa—the Cats lost to the Birmingham Barons four games to one. Future major leaguer Walt Dropo was the star of the series for Birmingham, clouting several long home runs.

Jack Lindsey:

"I tore up a knee against Shreveport. George Schmees was fast, and the whole series he was going after their infielders with hard slides. In retaliation, they went after Cats' infielders. On this occasion, instead of coming across second base to throw to first [on an attempted double play], I stayed behind second and cut loose a low throw. The runner ducked under the throw and rolled into my knee, stretching the ligaments.

"Those Cats' teams had some characters. Eddie Chandler was pitching for us one day, and in those times pitchers had to come up to hit. Eddie grounded easily to short, and as he ran to first he deliberately spiked the heel of the first baseman. I was up next, and the catcher whispered, 'Jack, stay loose.' I didn't know what he meant. After Grodziky, the pitcher, knocked me down twice, he finally hit me with his third pitch. When I got to first I was mad, hoping Bobby Bragan would give me the steal sign to second. He did, and I went in with cleats high and sliced their shortstop up good. I felt bad afterwards, but that's the way you played then."

Bobby Bragan:

"I was satisfied with the year. Irv Noren was voted the Texas League's most valuable player. Obviously, quite a few of my players were either going to move up in the Dodger system or else be sold or traded to rival organizations. Noren ended up in Washington. But the Dodger organization, I knew, was committed to Fort Worth and the Cats. There was never any doubt the players sent to Fort Worth for the 1949 season would be good ones."

They were. New Cats included Chico Carrasquel, an acrobatic shortstop; Joe Landrum, a steady starting pitcher; first baseman Preston Ward, who could hit with power; relief pitcher Billy Loes, eventually to become famous for claiming he missed a ground ball when the sun got in his eyes; and a young Nebraskan named Carroll Beringer, whose life and career Bragan has always said exemplified what the Fort Worth Cats were all about.

Carroll Beringer:

"I was 21 when I joined the Cats. I'd grown up on a farm in Nebraska. The school I went to there wasn't big enough to have a baseball team. My graduating class had three boys and three girls. But in the summer I turned 15, the nearby town of Columbus, a big town because it had 15,000 people, had an American Legion coach who asked me to try out for his team. He wanted me to play the outfield, but after he saw me swing a bat he decided I'd better pitch.

"Well, two years later the American Legion team from Omaha challenged the rest of the American Legion teams in the state to put together an all-star team and play them. I was picked to play. But my family was trying to make a living on our farm, and my Dad said he just couldn't spare me for the game because it was harvest time. My coach talked to him, just pleaded. Finally Dad said, 'Okay, Carroll can play, but you make sure he gets right back here afterwards so he can thresh the wheat.' So I pitched and beat Omaha 2-1 in a game that started at noon. By two-thirty I was back on the farm threshing the wheat.

"But I'd pitched well in that game. Word got around. The Dodgers had a tryout camp in Wichita and I got a chance to go. I did okay there, though I've always suspected the Dodger scout that signed me only did that because he enjoyed my mother's cooking so much. I was signed in 1945 for $90 a month, plus a $240 signing bonus. The scout threw in transportation money home for me at the end of my first season. Hell, even I knew I wasn't getting much money, but my feeling was, 'Hey, I can't believe somebody's gonna pay me to play baseball.'

The Cats paraded along Fort Worth Streets before challenging Birmingham in the 1948 Dixie Series (Special Collections, UTA).

Ted Williams crosses the plate after homering against the Cats in a 1947 exhibition game at LaGrave Field (Special Collections, UTA).

Chico Carrasquel Night, 1949 (Special Collections, UTA).

Bobby Bragan Night at LaGrave Field, 1949 (Special Collections, UTA).

"I was 18. The Dodgers sent me to a Class D team in Cambridge, Maryland, which was as low in the D League as you could get. It was a terrible team. I had a losing record for the season, and I could tell I just didn't have the kind of fastball you needed. My curve was my best pitch. After the season I took all the money I'd been able to save out of the bank, and then I sure was glad the scout had given me extra money to get home. Otherwise, I couldn't have afforded the train fare.

"The next year the Dodgers sent me back to Cambridge, and this time the team was pretty good. I won 25, lost six, and my winning percentage was only third best on the club! So the next year I was promoted to Newport News in a B League, and I went 13-8 there.

"So in 1949, I didn't really think I'd get lucky enough to go to Fort Worth. It was clear to everybody the Dodgers sent their top prospects there, and I wasn't one of those. But during spring training at Vero Beach I was placed with the Cats. It didn't necessarily mean anything. You could still be put on any team's roster. But Bobby was at least looking at me.

"Fort Worth played an exhibition game against the Houston Buffs. Bobby was catching. I got in to pitch. He called for a breaking ball when I was behind in the count. Most young pitchers want to go with their fastballs in those situations, but I threw my breaking ball and got the hitter out with it. As Bobby and I walked back to the dugout, he said, 'Carroll, you made my staff with that one pitch.'

"Golly, I thought Fort Worth was as big as New York City. I'd never lived anywhere that big. We came into town by train and I was just staring at all the buildings. I wondered how I'd ever learn my way around.

"I pitched in Fort Worth in 1949 and 1950, went into the military for two years and came back to pitch in Fort Worth through 1957. I figured out early on I wasn't getting any farther toward the majors. The Dodgers made that clear. Other pitchers got moved up, but I stayed and stayed. Sometimes I second guessed myself for not going to college and having some other, better career options. But, doggone it, I loved Fort Worth just like most of the other Cats players did. We were treated like family by the fans. I met my wife, Jimmie, here in 1950. She was a little girl, I thought. I went into the service, came back two years later, and she was all grown up. Lots of guys married Fort Worth girls. Jimmie and I got married in 1954 and settled here, so that made me prone to stay with the Cats, too. I actually did get moved to Montreal in Triple-A once, but my elbow gave me fits. I asked to come back to the warmer climate and my girlfriend Jimmie.

"And I wanted to come back to the Cats fans. Oh, those fans. We players loved 'em then and those of us still around love 'em to this day. It was a fabulous privilege to play professional baseball here. All of us on the team knew we were lucky, or at least we should have known it. You'd walk downtown and people would come up and want to talk baseball. And after Sunday games, it happened a lot that the whole club would be invited over to somebody's back yard for an ice-cream social. Don't laugh. That's the way things were.

"The fans really took care of us. They knew we were young kids hardly making any money. Those of us with families had to scrape every cent together. My wife Jimmie would sit in the stands at the games, and she became acquainted with this nice couple. When we started having our kids, every once in a while we'd open our front door in the morning and there would be a box from them with coats for the kids, or sometimes a check for $50. Fort Worth people were so good to us. We felt honored to talk with them after games, or to sign autographs if anybody asked."

Bobby Bragan:

"None of us ever would have thought to ask for money for our signatures. Never! Part of the thrill of being professional baseball players was being asked for autographs. In fact, when somebody did ask, you tried to sign quickly before they changed their minds and decided they didn't want your autograph after all."

Carroll Beringer:

"There's a lot more to the game than money."

Bobby Bragan:

"It was the players like Carroll Beringer who were the backbone of the best minor-league teams. Mr. Rickey knew this. You wanted a mix of players on these teams, some up-and-coming kids and some solid veterans who would provide steady leadership and contribute to a positive atmosphere in the clubhouse. As a manager, I wanted to have the Carroll Beringers on my teams. I knew, and they knew, the major leagues would not be in their futures. But with the Cats they still had fans who appreciated them, a good place to live and raise their families, and the fun of playing baseball and getting paid for it. Look at how many former Cats players stayed on and lived in this area. It wasn't coincidence."

Carroll Beringer:

"I look back on my days with the Fort Worth Cats and I cherish every one of them. Would I rather play now for the big bucks and miss what I had then with my teammates and those Fort Worth fans? Not for a minute."

The Cats dominated the Texas League during the 1949 season, but not everything worked perfectly for the franchise. On the night of May 15, most of LaGrave Field burned to the ground.

Dick Williams:

"I loved playing at LaGrave. Its old wooden stands were beautiful. In that '49 season I was rooming in Fort Worth with Joe Landrum, the pitcher. We boarded with a family. It was great. But Joe and I were both young and single, we liked sometimes to go out a little bit at night after games. So on this particular night we're at a party across the street from the fire station. All of a sudden all the fire trucks start racing off with their sirens going and Joe, kidding, says to me, 'Maybe the ballpark's burning.' And, of course, it was."

By dawn, LaGrave was a pile of smoking rubble except for some metal stands. The Cats were scheduled to play San Antonio. Folding chairs were set up around the field, and about 3,000 fans watched Landrum lose a 2-1 pitching duel. The Cats then went on a road trip that had to be extended while their field remained in ruins. Besides the fire, the Trinity River flooded, so the park was under equal parts of cinder and water. When it was finally ready for play again, the Cats were able to host the league's midseason all-star game on July 12. In that contest, the Cats took on a roster comprised of the best players from the league's other seven teams. Fort Worth won 2-1.

The 1949 season also marked the first television broadcast of a Cats game. The WBAP telecast was the first in the Southwest. The first major-league game was televised in 1939. Later, baseball's availability on television would be a major factor in the decline of the minor leagues. But the 1949 season was the minor-league system's heyday. Fifty-nine different leagues operated around the country, and the 16 major-league teams were still mostly confined to northeastern cities.

The Cats ruled the Southwest. At the end of the 1949 Texas League season, six of the Cats' eight regular starters had hit better than .300; third baseman Bob Bundy's .350 average led the club. Five players totaled double digits in steals. Four Cats' pitchers had earned-run averages under 3.00, and Landrum led all Texas League pitchers with 19 wins. Erskine had a 10-4 record before he was called up to the parent Brooklyn Dodgers. In all, the Cats were a team of remarkable balance.

Barbara Feagin (far left) and other contestants for the 1949 Miss Forth Worth Cats contest. Miss Feagin was the winner. (Mark Presswood Collection).

Barbara Feagin is escorted by Joe Landrum (Mark Presswood Collection).

Barbara Feagin is crowned Miss Fort Worth Cats, 1949 (Bobby Bragan Collection).

8

Cocky Cats

Nineteen forty-nine would be a banner year for the Panthers, and wins and pageantry went hand in hand. One highlight each season was the selection of "Miss Fort Worth Cats." In 1949, the winner was a girl from Weatherford.

Barbara Feagin Stroud:

"I was fourteen years old and living with my parents. The phone rang and this gentleman said, 'Barbara, this is Byron Scott.' I knew Byron Scott, as Weatherford was a town of about 8,000 citizens at that time and everyone knew everyone else. Mr. Scott went on to say that he was going to enter three girls from Weatherford in a beauty contest in Fort Worth. He said it was a contest to find a queen of the Fort Worth Cats, and wondered if I would consider becoming one of Weatherford's entries in the contest. I told him I would have to ask Mother, and I called her to the phone. I heard Mother say, 'I suppose so, but Barbara doesn't even own a bathing suit, so I'll have to see what we can come up with.' Mother then told me Mr. Scott wanted to take a picture of me in a bathing suit. My parents were pretty strict, and I didn't even own a pair of shorts. I borrowed a bathing suit top from one friend and a bathing suit bottom from another friend. Mother took me to Mr. and Mrs. Scott's home and sat there watching as he took some pictures of me. I did have my first pair of high heels, which I had talked my parents into buying for me to wear to church.

"Mr. Scott told us the names of two other girls from Weatherford who would be entering the contest, and his reason for entering us was publicity for his photography. He also told us he would give us prints of the pictures he took of me. We thanked him and went on home. Nothing at all was mentioned about my age or the age one needed to be to enter the contest.

"Lo and behold, in two days we received about ten phone calls in one afternoon. When we opened our *Fort Worth Star-Telegram,* there was my picture in the bathing suit in the sports section. Mother and I hadn't even told my Daddy about this as he wouldn't have liked it, and we had no idea my picture would appear in the paper.

"Daddy took it pretty well, but four of Mother's brothers phoned to let her know what they thought about it. They thought it was terrible for their niece's picture to appear in a bathing suit in the *Star-Telegram*. Mother and I were under the impression it was just a photography contest and whichever girl won would receive a nice piece of luggage as a prize. But to get to go to LaGrave Field—WOW!

"I really can't remember how many girls entered the contest, but I do remember there were three elimination nights. We were told that we were to appear at LaGrave Field at 7 p.m. one night for the first elimination contest. Mother bought me a bathing suit for the event. There were ten girls in the first elimination. The other two girls from Weatherford were eliminated. I evidently was still in the running. The next elimination included between 30 and 40 girls. In all, there were ten girls chosen as finalists. The Cats were the judges. And, as I later discovered, one was supposed to be at least seventeen years of age to enter. I was fourteen at the time Mr. Scott entered my picture, but I had turned fifteen in May of 1949. The finals were on September 7th.

"On that night, the finalists were called up individually with a Fort Worth Cat being an escort to each. We girls were then presented with a piece of luggage. We were taken into a room behind the dugout and instructed as to what to do once we were back on the field: Each girl would be introduced and escorted from the field one by one until there would be only one remaining. She would be Miss Fort Worth Cats of 1949. A Mr. Wallace Jay was giving these instructions, but I was not listening. I knew in the first place that I would not win, and I had just had a conversation with Beverly Wren, Miss Decatur. She came up to me and said, 'Can you believe that one of those girls from Weatherford who entered the contest was only fifteen years old? What audacity! I can't believe it!' That was one of the few times I had nothing to say. Joe Landrum had been selected by the sports writers as the Texas League Pitcher of the Year, and he was to be the escort for the Queen. A Lincoln convertible was to pick up the Queen and Landrum and drive them around the infield to the acknowledgment of the crowd. Of course, I heard nothing of this as I was trying to think of some answer to give Beverly.

"Finally, there were only two girls remaining on the field. When the announcer started to say something I started to slowly walk off. Then he announced the other girl's name. She evidently thought she had won it, because I looked up and she knocked away her escort's arm as she stormed off the field. And there stood this fifteen-year-old Weatherford moron not having any idea what I was supposed to do. Joe presented me to Bobby Bragan at home plate, and he crowned me Queen. I was interviewed at the plate, and all I can recall was their telling me two teams' names and asking me, when the Cats went to the Dixie Series, which of the teams I would rather that they play. I had no earthly idea, as this was only the second professional baseball game I had been to in my entire life. The first one was the night I competed in the first contest elimination. I can remember that I must have responded with the name of the wrong team, because many in the audience booed.

"It was lots of fun. The Weatherford merchants made quite a big deal out of it. They went together and gave me a new wardrobe and more luggage. The Cats presented me with roses and corsages, and I was allowed to take as many guests to any games as I wanted.

Pitcher George Dockins, who served as an undefeated interim manager for the Cats in 1948 (Mark Presswood Collection).

Joe Macko, 1958 (Special Collections, UTA).

Wedding bells for four Cats players at home plate, La Grave Field. The date is August 21, 1950 (Bobby Bragan Collection).

Carroll and Jimmie Beringer (Mark Presswood Collection).

"I also accompanied the team on a few road trips. Our first was to Shreveport, Louisiana. Mother, of course, was my chaperone. We flew—my first time in a plane. I was even interviewed on the radio. On Sunday morning Chico Carrasquel, who was trying to learn to speak and read English, sat in the lobby of the hotel with Mother and me and we read the Sunday funny papers to him, trying to explain them. Mother had been a schoolteacher and she would point out a word in the cartoon strip, repeat it and have Chico repeat it. He was so eager to learn.

"While we were in Shreveport, Cal Abrams of the Cats bought me a little bottle of Evening in Paris perfume at the hotel. He gave it to me while Mother and I were trying to teach Chico how to read the funny papers. I still have that perfume bottle.

"The most embarrassing part of being Miss Fort Worth Cats was when my principal insisted that I invite Bobby Bragan to Weatherford to speak to one of our school assemblies. I did, dreading it like the plague. For there I was, in the ninth grade at a junior high school. I've always wondered what Bobby thought, since I was supposed to be seventeen years old, and yet there I was, only in the ninth grade."

Shortstop Chico Carrasquel became a special fan favorite. On July 25, the team and its supporters held "Chico Carrasquel Night" at LaGrave Field.

Dick Williams:

"It was a big thing for Chico. He had to leave his family, his wife, behind in Venezuela and he really missed them. The fans and John Reeves got the money together to bring them to Fort Worth for the rest of the season. They were kept out of sight ahead of time, and finally they were put in a car and the car was driven onto the field. Chico got all excited because he thought he was being given a car. You should have seen his face when his wife got out and they drove the car away! But I guess he ended up being even more pleased seeing her."

The Cats won the Texas League pennant by 10 games over second-place Tulsa. They clinched the title when they beat Tulsa in the first game of a doubleheader. With first place secured, Bragan used the second game to demonstrate his wicked sense of humor.

Carroll Beringer:

"All season long I'd been asking Bobby to let me start a game. He'd always tell me to be quiet and stay in the bullpen. Well, we clinch the pennant in the first game that day against Tulsa, and while everybody's shouting and celebrating Bobby walks over to me in the clubhouse, hands me a ball, and says real nasty-like, 'I listened to you bitch about starting all year. Now go get 'em.' So I start the game. Right away somebody gets on, and next thing, my catcher throws the ball halfway past the centerfielder, and it gets bad. I mean, bad. I'm not sure how many runs I gave up, but it was a lot. And Bragan just sat on the bench laughing at me. He wouldn't take me out of the game. Finally he comes and says, 'You ready?' and I say, 'Bobby, why don't you go back to the bench and leave me in until they get 20?' By the time he took me out, well, before that game my ERA was about 2.00, maybe less, and by the time I was back in the clubhouse after my one and only start, that ERA was going on 4.00.

"And, of course, the whole train ride back to Fort Worth Bobby kept coming up to me and saying, 'Did you have fun? Did you enjoy your start?' To this day he gets on me about it."

Bragan, his cocky team and the equally cocky Cats fans all expected Fort Worth to waltz through the Texas League play-offs and crush their Southern Association opponent in the Dixie Series. After all, old-timers were favorably comparing the '49 Cats to Jake Atz's best teams of the 1920s.

Things went according to plan in the first play-off round. Fort Worth handily dispatched Shreveport in five games; Tulsa edged Oklahoma City in six, so the Cats met Tulsa for the Texas League championship. The Oilers were tougher in the play-offs than they had been in the regular season. The Cats won the first two games, but Tulsa won the next three. A game away from elimination, Fort Worth beat Tulsa 1-0 at LaGrave Field, setting up a climactic seventh game that was also played in Fort Worth.

Bobby Bragan:

"That game remains my worst baseball memory. I still think about it. It still hurts. We were tied with Tulsa going into the last of the ninth inning. Dick Williams led off for us and hit a triple. He was held at third, but the relay throw came within an inch of bouncing into our dugout. We would have won the game right there. But it didn't happen.

"So Dick is on third, and Chico Carrasquel comes up. The Tulsa manager has him walked intentionally. I'm up next, and I'm walked intentionally, too. Al Vincent, the Tulsa manager, did this to set up the force play at home. But we now had the bases loaded with nobody out, and the game is in our hands. As I got to first, the umpire there congratulated me for having the game and the title wrapped up.

"I thought about taking myself out of the game, going in to coach third base and maybe putting on the squeeze bunt. I meant to do this. I even walked toward our dugout. As I got there, I looked right in the eyes of Andy Skurski, a very good hitter. He'd been our best pinch hitter all year. But Jack Lindsey was due up, and for some reason I let him hit and kept Skurski on the bench. Jack grounded to short, and the shortstop forced Dick Williams at home. One out now. The bases were still loaded. I still had Skurski available, but instead I called for Walt Sessi to bat for our pitcher. Sessi grounded to the second baseman. Carrasquel was forced at home. Two out. Now Cal Abrams, our leadoff hitter, comes up, and he hits a long fly ball to

The ticket office, LaGrave Field, mid-1950s (Mark Presswood Collection).

Carl Erskine, pitcher in 1948 (Mark Presswood Collection).

The 1950 Cats (Bobby Bragan Collection).

Bragan disputes a call with umpire Len Roberts. Cats' shortstop Rudy Rufer joins in (Bobby Bragan Collection).

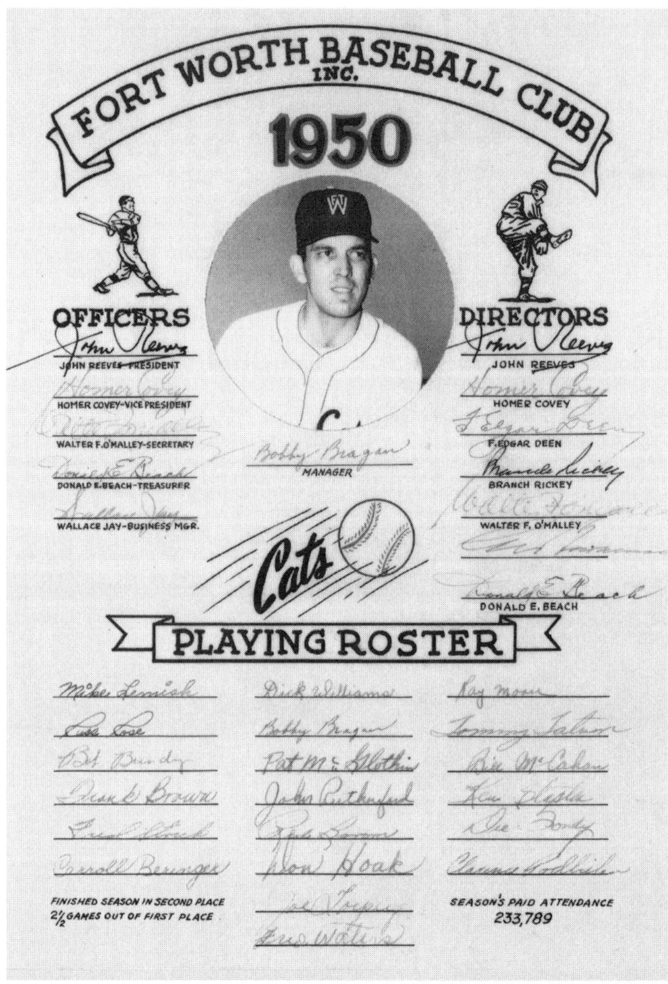

Award plaque given to Bragan by team President John Reeves in 1950 (Bobby Bragan Collection).

left. With less than two outs, it's a sacrifice fly and the winning run scores. Instead, it's just the third out.

"Now I'm still tied and have to bring in a relief pitcher. I choose Joe Landrum, and in the eleventh inning he gives up a single to Tulsa's leadoff hitter. Al Vincent has the next batter sacrifice him to second, and I order the next Tulsa hitter walked to set up the double play.

"Joe Adcock comes up with men on first and second, and he hits the ball over the left field wall into the Trinity River. We don't score in the bottom half of the inning, and the Oilers are champions. What a sad end to a great season, and all because I made the wrong decisions in the bottom of the ninth. For many days I was inconsolable."

Even so, fans believed the '49 Cats were one of the greatest minor league teams ever assembled. Bragan thought so, too.

Bobby Bragan:

"The '49 Fort Worth Cats were a fine, fine team. I would say if we played 10 games against today's Texas Rangers, we would win four games and maybe five. The Rangers of today would be better athletes. We would have the advantage of baseball experience and knowledge. My Cats didn't make silly mistakes like the major leaguers of today."

Mark Presswood:

"I don't think the '48 or '49 Cats could have compared to today's major-league players. They were good, solid ballplayers, but athletes today are much stronger and faster. Still, the '49 Cats match up favorably with any other minor-league team anybody else ever put together. For one thing, Chico Carrasquel, the shortstop, was just the best at that position ever to play in Fort Worth. Preston Ward was at first, Dick Williams was the centerfielder, Cal Abrams was in left, the pitchers included Eddie Chandler, Carl Erskine, Joe Landrum, Billy Loes. Show me another comparable minor-league team. Tulsa did win the seven-game playoff, but that's baseball. The best team doesn't always win a short series."

One drawback to the Cats' 1949 success, of course, was that almost all the team's players would move on and up in the Dodger organization. Among Bragan's eight position starters during that year, only Dick Williams returned to Fort Worth for the 1950 season—and he didn't want to be there.

Dick Williams:

"After my great season, I fully expected to be promoted to Triple-A and Montreal. At spring training when I found I'd still be a Cat, I requested an audience

Outfielder Edwin "Duke" Snider, future Hall of Fame member, in 1946 (Mark Presswood Collection).

Second baseman Wally Fiala, 1948 (Mark Presswood Collection).

First baseman Dee Fondy, 1948 (Mark Presswood Collection).

Joe Landrum, pitcher, 1949 (Mark Presswood Collection).

with Mr. Rickey. And that's really what it was, an audience with royalty. Mr. Rickey said, 'Son, we have high hopes for you. Now, the salary we're paying you should be sufficient; you're single. You can go straight from Fort Worth to the big leagues.' So in 1950 in Fort Worth I hit .300 on the nose, and the next year I did go right up to the big leagues with Brooklyn."

Rickey believed in staying in close contact with his managers, though he preferred inexpensive means of doing so. At one point, he notified all 21 managers of Brooklyn farm teams that they should not send telegrams to his office in Brooklyn if special delivery mail would do for less important messages. In fact, Rickey urged, they should use regular mail if at all possible.

Ten days later, Rickey sent Bragan a telegram inquiring, "Can you go with your present infield?" Bragan, wanting to impress the boss by spending as little money on a return telegram as possible, wired back a one-word answer: "Yes."

When Rickey received the telegram, he couldn't recall his original question. He cabled, "Yes, what?"

The ever-polite Bragan wired back, "Yes, SIR."

Though Rickey had taken away Preston Ward, Cal Abrams, Carl Erskine and other stalwarts, he sent Bragan good players in their place. The 1950 Cats' infield included future major leaguers Dee Fondy on first and Don Hoak at third. Williams was back in centerfield and Landrum and Beringer were holdovers from the previous season's pitching staff.

There was also continuity in the warm relationship between fans and players.

Bobby Bragan:

"Mr. Reeves believed in promotions that brought the paying customers and the Cats together. We might have watermelon night, and after the game players vould sit in the stands sharing watermelon with the fans. Talent Night was always great fun. I recall Carl Erskine standing on the back of a flatbed truck and singing at the top of his lungs.

"There were no real problems with discipline, besides Dick Williams sometimes talking back. I was never awakened in the middle of the night by a phone call informing me a player was drunk and in jail. I remember one thing: The parents of a girl in Houston contacted the club to say a Cats player had gotten their daughter pregnant. This was the one time I felt I had to call Mr. Reeves and consult him about such a thing. Mr. Reeves made a trip to Houston and met with the woman and her parents as well as the player. He quietly agreed to pay for an abortion. This is the only time I can recall such a serious problem.

"The players and the writers also got on well. Blackie Sherrod was one of the writers. No one then in the newspaper business cared to write about a player's private life. They stuck to the stuff on the field. And there was more going on than just baseball. During the 1950 season we had four players get married at home plate. Second baseman Joe Torpey, pitcher Johnny Rutherford, third baseman Don Hoak and shortstop Russ Rose. I was Torpey's best man. Blackie Sherrod was best man for Rutherford or Rose. I believe *LIFE* magazine did a story on the event."

What Cats fans didn't realize was that they almost didn't have a team to support. After LaGrave Field burned, the Dodgers had to decide whether to keep their top Double-A team in Fort Worth, which would entail the expense of rebuilding the stadium, or move the franchise somewhere with an available ballpark. Rickey wanted to keep the Cats where they were; the team remained.

But Branch Rickey didn't stay in Brooklyn.

Bobby Bragan:

"For years, Mr. Rickey and Walter O'Malley had each owned 25 per cent of the Dodgers. The other 50 per cent was divided between two other owners. Gradually, these owners aligned themselves with Walter O'Malley. Mr. Rickey did not want to remain where he was clearly not in charge. Eventually, he sold his Dodger stock to O'Malley for, I believe, $1 million, a fabulous sum in those days.

"There was never any question Branch Rickey would remain in baseball. I'm sure there were teams lined up offering him whatever job he wanted in their organizations. He eventually accepted a position as general manager of the Pittsburgh Pirates. Like everyone else in Fort Worth, I wished him well. My career had prospered because of him. I never considered, though, begging him to take me to the Pittsburgh organization with him. He was, I suppose I could say, my mentor, but he taught many other people besides me. My personal goal remained the same—to work my way up the Brooklyn minor-league ladder and eventually manage the Dodgers."

In 1950, the Cats finished second instead of first and Texas League attendence dropped by 350,000. In *The Texas League*, author Bill O'Neal theorizes that the advent of television in most homes, more children playing Little League baseball in the evenings and home air-conditioning to combat sweltering Texas summers combined to keep people away from the pro ballparks. From this season forward, minor leagues would disappear one by one; those that remained often had to scramble for enough franchises to get through the year. Even Fort Worth would eventually find itself switching leagues.

In 1950, though, the Cats had to eat former manager Roger Hornsby's dust. Hornsby had returned as manager of the Beaumont Roughnecks, which was now a New York Yankee affiliate. The Roughnecks finished first by a wide margin. Fort Worth was still fun to watch; they earned an 88-64 record by emphasizing team speed. Nine players stole 13 or more bases.

Bobby Bragan:

> "One other thing I remember about 1950 is the umpires. They got along better with the players in those days, though I was already acquiring a reputation for correcting their bad calls more forceably than they might have preferred. One such umpire was Frenchy Arceneaux, a fine gentleman blessed with reasonable patience. On one occasion he called a strike on my first baseman, Dee Fondy. Fondy whirled and snapped at the umpire, 'That's two in a row you've missed, Frenchy!' And this fine man replied, 'In that case, Dee, let me apologize for both of 'em right now!'
>
> "I love that story, and it's true."

In 1951 there was less joy at LaGrave Field. This time Bragan's Cats could only finish tied for fourth in the league with Beaumont. The two teams played a single-elimination game to see which would advance to the post-season play-offs. Beaumont won, and the Cats went home. Despite an 84-77 record, the Cats still had some standouts. Shortstop Billy Hunter remains one of Bragan's favorites among all the players he ever managed. Torpey and Lindsey were still there, and left fielder Gino Cimoli led the Texas League with 12 triples. Like Roberto Clemente and Elroy Face, Cimoli was a Dodger farmhand who wouldn't escape Branch Rickey's continued attention; the Mahatma eventually made deals to bring all three into the Pirate organization.

Bragan also had the brief pleasure of managing his own brother, but Jimmy Bragan, an infielder, just couldn't handle Double-A pitching. Regretfully, his older brother demoted him to a Dodger Single-A farm team in Newport News, Virginia. A few weeks later, Bragan decided he also needed to demote catcher Norm Sherry. He called Sherry over and said simply, "When you get to Newport News, say hello to Jimmy for me." Sherry got the unwelcome message.

In 1952, the Cats did better, finishing second during the regular season to rival Dallas before losing to Shreveport in the first play-off round. The

Bobby Bragan brawls with Frank Biscan of San Antonio (Special Collections, UTA).

George Schmees is greeted after homering in 1948 (Special Collections, UTA).

Chico Carrasquel avoids a tag at first (Special Collections, UTA).

1952 Texas League season is best remembered for the presence of the league's first black player. Dave Hoskins won 22 games for Dallas despite not being allowed by state rules to compete against Shreveport in Lousiana.

Cats fans recall 1952 for another reason. It was Bobby Bragan's last with the Fort Worth Cats.

Bobby Bragan:

"With Mr. Rickey gone, the Dodgers decided to remove Mr. Reeves as the Cats' president. I felt they had no cause to do this. I learned of his dismissal during the Texas League off-season; I was out of the country managing a club in Cuba. Immediately, I called Buzzie Bavasi, an executive in the Dodger front office, to ask if it was true. He said it was, so I took a deep breath and informed him I no longer wanted to manage the Fort Worth Cats or to remain in the Brooklyn organization.

This was hard for me to say to Buzzie. My family and I loved Fort Worth. I had no intention of moving out of town even though I would no longer manage the Cats. Buzzie tried to talk me out of it. At one point, he even said he just couldn't believe I thought more of one man than I did the Brooklyn Dodgers. I responded that, if he preferred, I would put my request in writing to be traded or sold to another organization. As a seasoned player-manager, I knew I would have value.

"A few days later, Bavasi called to say I'd been traded to the Pittsburgh Pirates. Mr. Rickey then named me player-manager of the Hollywood Stars, a Triple-A team in the Pacific Coast League. I was pleased with the promotion; moving up to Triple-A placed me just one step away from becoming a major-league manager. But I hated to leave Fort Worth; I just couldn't remain with the Cats without Mr. Reeves, a man who had been very good to me—and very good for the team. The Dodgers were wrong to let him go."

Bragan's impulsive decision led to immediate career advancement, but it probably hurt him in the long run. He managed the Hollywood Stars for three seasons. In 1956, Rickey was removed as general manager of the Pirates. As his last act with the team, he named Bragan manager. Bragan didn't mesh well with some of Pittsburgh's talented young players; his sarcasm hurt their feelings, and he was fired before the end of the 1957 season. His next big-league stop was even briefer; he was fired by the Cleveland Indians after running the club for just half of 1958.

For a short time, Bragan returned to the Dodgers, managing Spokane for the remainder of 1958 and all of 1959. During this time, he convinced a shortstop named Maury Wills to switch-hit; that proved to be Wills' ticket to the majors.

In 1960, Bragan coached third for the Dodgers. He left to join the expansion Houston Colt .45s, working in the team's front office in 1961 and then serving as its bullpen coach in 1962. From 1963 through part of 1966 he managed the Braves in Milwaukee and Atlanta, but was fired when, once again, many of his players failed to respond to his sarcasm and insistence on having everything done his way. There was added pressure while he ran the Braves; Bragan found himself caught in the middle of the team's highly controversial move from Wisconsin to Georgia. Though he had other offers, Bobby Bragan never managed again.

Had he remained with the Cats instead of insisting on a trade following the dismissal of John Reeves, many believe Bragan would eventually have managed the Dodgers. Brooklyn, and later Los Angeles, believed in long-term contracts for managers who worked their way up through the team's farm system. First Walter Alston, then Tom Lasorda, spent years at the helm and were supported through good seasons and bad. (Current Dodger ownership no longer adheres to this philosophy.)

Carroll Beringer:

> "Everybody expected Bobby would one day manage the Dodgers. Everybody. And he'd have been a big succcess at it, too. See, when Bobby went on to other organizations he wanted everything done the Dodger way, and these other teams just didn't get it. Bobby was always impatient. His greatest gift was the ability to teach, but you'd have to say his weakness was saying things that maybe hurt more than he realized they did. With the Dodgers, you see, he wouldn't have been so frustrated by players who didn't know how to or just didn't care to play the game right. I think he might have cost himself a place in the Hall of Fame when he quit the Dodgers. Alston and Lasorda got in, you know. And Bobby was every bit as good a baseball man as either one of 'em."

Opening day, 1951—Owen Martinez, business manager, Ezra Bland, groundskeeper, John Reeves, team president, Bobby Bragan, manager, Steve Crooks, concession manger (Bobby Bragan Collection).

Bobby Bragan, Judge Clarence "Big Boy" Kraft and Branch Rickey, Jr. (Bobby Bragan Collection).

Bobby Bragan's Bible class (Bobby Bragan Collection).

9

The Beginning of the End

Before the start of the 1953 major-league baseball season, the Boston Braves moved to Milwaukee. Though the Braves had been in Boston since 1871 as charter members of the National Association, the city clearly preferred the American League's Red Sox. When the Braves gained National League permission to move, Milwaukee seemed like a logical choice. Nearby Chicago had the Cubs to provide a regional major-league rivalry, and the minor-league Milwaukee Brewers had always been able to draw good crowds. Since National League teams were already including Chicago in their travel schedule, Milwaukee could be included on those road trips, which were still made by train. When the Braves came to town, the minor-league Brewers had to move. But Milwaukee baseball fans clearly preferred the big leaguers; not only did the Braves finish second in the National League in 1953, they also set a league attendence record of 1,800,000. Of course, they offered an attractve team on the field, with Warren Spahn, Eddie Mathews, Lew Burdette and Bob Buhl. Hank Aaron would join the team in 1954.

Other major-league team owners were impressed, especially those whose clubs weren't drawing well in their current cities. The tactic of picking a new hometown was obvious: select a city or region with a strong minor-league history. Potential locations were still considered geographically limited roughly to Boston in the North, Milwaukee and Chicago in the upper Midwest, St. Louis in the central Midwest and Washington, D.C., in the South.

The St. Louis Browns were the next to move, abandoning St. Louis to the far more successful Cardinals. The Browns chose Baltimore, renaming themselves the Orioles in honor of the minor-league club that had flourished there. Again, it made geographic sense. American League teams already played the Washington Senators.

Down in Fort Worth, the Cats and their fans didn't realize the Boston-Milwaukee and St. Louis-Baltimore shifts were only the beginning of fran-

The 1955 starting lineup from left to right: Bobby Dolan, Harry Schwegman, Dick Willams Calvin Felix, Frank Marchio, Danny Ozark, Sparky Anderson, Joe Pignatano and Mike Lemish (Mark Presswood Collection).

Maury Wills, 1955 (Mark Presswood Collection).

chise shifts in the major leagues that would eventually eliminate most minor-league strongholds.

At LaGrave Field, the biggest news was Bobby Bragan's departure. Max Macon was the new Cats' manager. He'd last only a season—it would be years before any Fort Worth skipper would return for a second go-'round—while guiding the club to an 82-72 record, good for third place in the Texas League. The 1953 Cats were largely forgettable; Beringer and Rutherford were the holdovers from the Bragan days, along with Jimmy Bragan, back for a second unsuccessful stint. First baseman Danny Ozark batted .300 with 23 home runs; third baseman Jim Baxes had 107 runs batted in; second baseman Spook Jacobs scored 102 runs and stole 28 bases. Fort Worth was eliminated in the first round of the post-season play-offs.

In 1954, Ozark and Beringer were back, but not Macon. The new Cats manager was Al Vincent, admired by his players for his intelligence but not as much by his employers for his won-loss record. The 81-80 Cats were fourth in the league despite new pitching star Karl Spooner's league-leading 21 wins and 262 strikeouts. Fort Worth beat Shreveport in the first play-off round, but lost to Houston in the championship match up.

The 1955 Cats were memorable, but not for their poor 77-84 won-loss record for manager Tommy Holmes. This was the season the first black players wore Fort Worth uniforms. Shortstop Maury Wills was a starter; outfielder Eddie Moore saw spot duty.

Dick Williams:

"I'd gotten injured, and in 1955 the Dodgers had me back in Fort Worth. The way I remember it, everybody at LaGrave was great to Maury and Eddie, lots of fan support. Where they had problems was against a few teams on the road, teams that didn't have any black players on their rosters. Waco, I remember, was pretty bad."

Maury Wills:

"I played for the Cats in 1955. I was the team's first black player, and one of the few in the Texas League. I was just a young kid, 23, I suppose, and emotionally a very young 23. I'd been born and raised in the projects of Washington, D.C., with everybody around me black. My first couple years in pro ball after signing with the Dodgers were spent in upstate New York, where everybody wasn't black, but the prejudice wasn't nearly the same as it was in the South.

"I was thrilled to sign with Brooklyn. All the black kids wanted to sign with Brooklyn because of Jackie Robinson. He was still playing for the Dodgers, so before

I left town to go to D ball I bragged to my hometown buddies that in two years I'd be in Brooklyn playing with Jackie. Ha!

"Well, after those seasons in New York, all of a sudden I was in Fort Worth, Texas, where fans would cheer me when I was on the field and after games didn't want me to sit next to them on the city bus. Hey, by law I couldn't sit with them on the bus. I couldn't stay in hotels with my teammates on road trips. The hotels wouldn't take me. This was my first time to ever have to really live under such conditions, and I responded with the worst year of my career.

"I remember nights in Fort Worth when I hadn't gotten a hit, when I'd played badly and later been treated like somebody second-class on the street, and I'd lie in bed and think I just couldn't take it anymore. I can't really give you the specifics of some of the worst things that happened. Over the years I've been able to push them completely out of my mind."

Dick Williams:

"At that time at LaGrave, they still had special outfield seating for blacks. If you weren't white, you had to sit in that one outfield section—and for sure, nobody white sat there."

Maury Wills:

"For some of the guys on the team, it was the first time they'd had a black teammate. Maybe I made a positive contribution to their lives by showing them we were really all alike. We were playing because we loved the game. We couldn't play for the money because there was no money. You made a few hundred dollars a month. I don't think any player today would stand for having the conditions we had, no money especially. I know when the '55 season was over I was ready to get out of Fort Worth. There was $250 in my pocket. I'd saved every cent I could the whole time I was there and that was all I had. I thought I had a deal with the Cats to pay for my transportation home, but when the season was over they didn't come up with it. So I bought a car for $200, an old Buick, and drove as fast as I could back to Washington, D.C., using the $50 left over from the car purchase for gas."

Dick Williams:

"I think Maury got frustrated because he couldn't hit with the Cats. It seemed like he could field anything, but he couldn't hit at all. When he finally became a big-league star years later, it came as a complete surprise to me, but it all turned around for him in 1958, I think, when the Dodgers sent him to their farm club in Spokane. Who do you think was managing there and taught Maury what he needed to finally succeed, which was switch-hitting? Why, it was Bobby Bragan."

Bobby Bragan:

"It still breaks my heart to think of Maury being unhappy while in Fort Worth. I'm glad he's often come back to the city since, and I believe he has come to like it.

Outfielder Don Demeter, who led the Texas league in home runs in 1956 (Mark Presswood Collection).

Sparky Anderson, 1955 (Mark Presswood Collection).

Dick Williams, 1955 (Mark Presswood Collection).

First baseman Jim Gentile, 1956 (Mark Presswood Collection).

Black players, particularly those who played in the minor leagues in the South and Southwest, had tough times in the mid-'50s. Some black players had become stars in the major leagues—Willie Mays, Hank Aaron, Larry Doby, Roy Campanella, of course Jackie Robinson—but there were still far more white players. It became a practice with many major-league clubs to send their best black prospects to minor-league teams in the North and Northeast. The Giants sent Willie Mays to Minneapolis, for instance.

"Fans learned to change over time. Fort Worth fans did not automatically hate what we might call minority players. Look at Chico Carrasquel. They loved Chico in Fort Worth. But he was Venezuelan. In Texas, the black players took the brunt of any racial abuse. Possibly Maury could have helped his cause if he had hit .300 in 1955 instead of .202. That's not fair, of course, but still maybe the way it could have been. And it is hard to think of maybe being asked for autographs by the same people who later would expect you to go to the back of the bus. I salute Maury and all the black minor-league players of that era for their courage."

Dick Williams:

"By the way, Eddie Moore, the other black player on that '55 team, ended up as a guard for the Dodgers at Chavez Ravine after Brooklyn moved to Los Angeles. See, the organization always looked out for its former players."

The 1955 Cats were remarkable in another way. Five players from that roster—Danny Ozark, George "Sparky" Anderson, Maury Wills, Dick Williams and Norm Sherry—went on to become major-league managers. Joe Pignatano and Carroll Beringer had long stints as coaches with major-league clubs. But with the exception of Williams, who had a .317 average and 24 homers, these future managers and coaches didn't play well in the season they were together in Fort Worth.

Cats' management tried to make up for poor team performance with extra efforts to charm the local fans.

Ann King Patrick and Jan King Rhinefort:

"We had moved away, but in 1955 we came back to Fort Worth. We now were in our early twenties. We didn't have much money, but L.D. Lewis, the Cats' general manager, would make sure we would win the evening's lucky number contest sometimes by selling us just the right program with that night's winning number in it. That way we would win tickets to another game. Mr. Lewis was such a nice man."

The 1956 Cats did a little better. Clay Bryant was the new manager; his single year at the Fort Worth helm resulted in an 84-70 record, good for third place in the regular season. For a change, the Cats won with their bats. First baseman Jim Gentile hit 40 homers, but didn't even lead his own team. Centerfielder Don Demeter did that, hitting 41. Demeter's total would have led the Texas League in six of the last seven seasons, but it wasn't enough in '56—Shreveport's Ken Guettler hit 62. Despite Gentile and Demeter, Fort Worth lost to Dallas in the first round of the post season.

In 1957, the Cats were a bad team. Lee Handley, the latest manager, didn't have much material to work with. Old reliable Carroll Beringer won 11 games, and while Larry Sherry could only post a 10-10 record, he still led the Texas League with 146 strikeouts. But no hitter drove in more than 67 runs or scored more than 74. With a 70-84 season mark, the team didn't need to worry about qualifying for the post-season play-offs.

Over the winter, the Cats and Fort Worth baseball fans had other things on their minds. Major league baseball had made another land grab, this one all the way to the West Coast—with a stop in Fort Worth on the way.

1963 Dallas-Fort Worth Rangers (Mark Presswood Collection).

1963 (Mark Presswood Collection).

10
The End of the Cats

Brooklyn Dodgers owner Walter O'Malley wanted a new stadium; 32,000-seat Ebbets Field, built in 1913, was in need of major repairs, and its location in the middle of a city block had always limited parking for the paying customers. Parking had become critical for Brooklyn fans, because New York City's demographics were changing. More families were moving out to the suburbs, and, if they wanted to come see the Dodgers, they would drive back into the city in their sedans. Without convenient parking, they might decide to just stay home and watch baseball on television.

O'Malley commissioned architect Buckminster Fuller to design a spacious stadium complete with dome, so that Brooklyn games could no longer be rained out. O'Malley even had the perfect site for the ballpark, a choice location on Brooklyn's Flatbush Avenue. But the city would not grant permission for construction to begin.

Walter O'Malley was a self-made man who had acquired controlling interest in the Dodgers over many years. He was less a baseball fan than a canny executive with an eye for the financial bottom line. If Brooklyn didn't want his Dodgers to have a fancy new stadium with lots of parking, O'Malley knew there would be other cities grateful for the chance to give the club just about anything it wanted. That meant relocation, which until 1953 had been almost unthinkable for a major-league team. Tradition, after all, was what baseball was supposed to be about. But the Braves had moved from Boston to Milwaukee and done well. Baltimore supported the Browns-turned-Orioles far better than St. Louis had done. Even the perennial sad-sack Philadelphia Athletics sold over a million tickets in their first season after moving to Kansas City.

Now, O'Malley decided, it was time for major-league baseball to push the edges of the relocation envelope. Air travel between the East and West coasts suddenly made it possible for ball clubs to get anywhere in the country in a day; the limits of train travel no longer applied. And

California had always been prime baseball country. Particularly in the 1940s and '50s, perhaps the richest of all minor leagues was the Pacific Coast League. The massive state of California provided lots of regional territory for almost innumerable teams, and such clubs as the Hollywood Stars, Los Angeles Angels and San Francisco Seals flourished in the PCL. There was just an extra glamor to California teams. The Marx Brothers, Frank Sinatra, Cary Grant, Jayne Mansfield, Milton Berle and other TV, music and movie stars regularly attended Stars and Angels games. Players loved living and competing on the West Coast. A running joke among major-league general managers was that their best prospects shouldn't be placed on Pacific Coast League teams for fear the athletes would refuse to leave the area after promotion to a big-league club.

Bob Bluthardt:

> "By the early 1950s it was obvious major-league baseball was going to move West and South, West first. The success of the Pacific Coast League had everything to do with that."

Two California cities intrigued O'Malley most. San Francisco and Los Angeles were clearly the places most suited to major-league franchises. They combined large populations, citizens with plenty of disposable income and long histories of supporting the minor-league teams based there. That bringing the Dodgers to one of those two cities meant its minor-league team would be displaced didn't bother Walter O'Malley at all. He had ideas about that, too.

O'Malley met with officials from both cities. Those from Los Angeles made particularly telling arguments. New York City was obviously Yankee country, they noted. The Dodgers would always be second in any municipal consideration there. The New York Giants, Brooklyn's traditional National League rival, was a club suffering from fan and city neglect, too. Los Angeles wanted the Dodgers, would love the Dodgers, would help O'Malley build a showcase stadium. That was what the Dodger owner wanted to hear; he chose Los Angeles as his team's new home.

But there were still complications; O'Malley had to do more before approaching National League owners with a request to move. Above all, if the Dodgers were the National League's only West Coast club there would be terrible problems scheduling games. It made little sense to fly a team to

Los Angeles for a three-game series and then fly it all the way back to Philadelphia or Chicago or Pittsburgh. There would have to be a second West Coast club. That would mean visiting teams could stay in California for a week. The Dodgers would be able to develop a new regional rivalry. Whichever club joined the Dodgers in California ought to relocate in San Francisco, since the Los Angeles-San Francisco civic rivalry was on a par with that between New York and Boston or Fort Worth and Dallas.

O'Malley knew just who he wanted to invite to San Francisco.

Horace Stoneham, owner of the New York Giants, loved baseball the way O'Malley loved money. But he didn't love the way New York fans and city officials were treating him. The Polo Grounds, home of the Giants since 1891, was decaying faster than Ebbets Field. But the city wasn't willing to fix it up. Even though Willie Mays still patrolled center field, fans weren't coming to Giants' games. Sadly, Stoneham began to consider moving his team to Minneapolis, where the Giants had enjoyed a long affiliation with the minor-league Millers. O'Malley talked Stoneham out of that. Why not relocate instead to beautiful San Francisco, where city officials would roll out the financial red carpet just as Los Angeles leaders had done for O'Malley? There was the added bonus of keeping the Dodgers-Giants rivalry going. Stoneham liked the idea.

Now came the final problem for O'Malley and Stoneham to solve. Baseball still operated under regional restrictions. No team, even major-league clubs as distinguished as the Brooklyn Dodgers and New York Giants, could arbitrarily pack up and move into somebody else's territory. The Chicago Cubs operated the Los Angeles Angels, while the Boston Red Sox owned the San Francisco Seals. Neither would simply let the Dodgers or Giants come in and literally close their successful minor-league franchises down. So O'Malley negotiated trades. Stoneham would give the Red Sox his Minneapolis farm team in exchange for territorial rights to San Francisco and shutting down the Seals. O'Malley himself would get rid of the Angels and placate the Cubs by swapping them the famous Fort Worth Cats. Officials of the Millers, Seals, Angels and Cats, let alone their fans, were not consulted. In May 1957, National League owners approved the proposed relocations of the Dodgers and Giants. When fans in New York protested vehemently, often claiming the two teams were betraying the children who worshipped them, Stoneham repied, "I feel sorry for the kids, but I haven't seen much of their fathers lately."

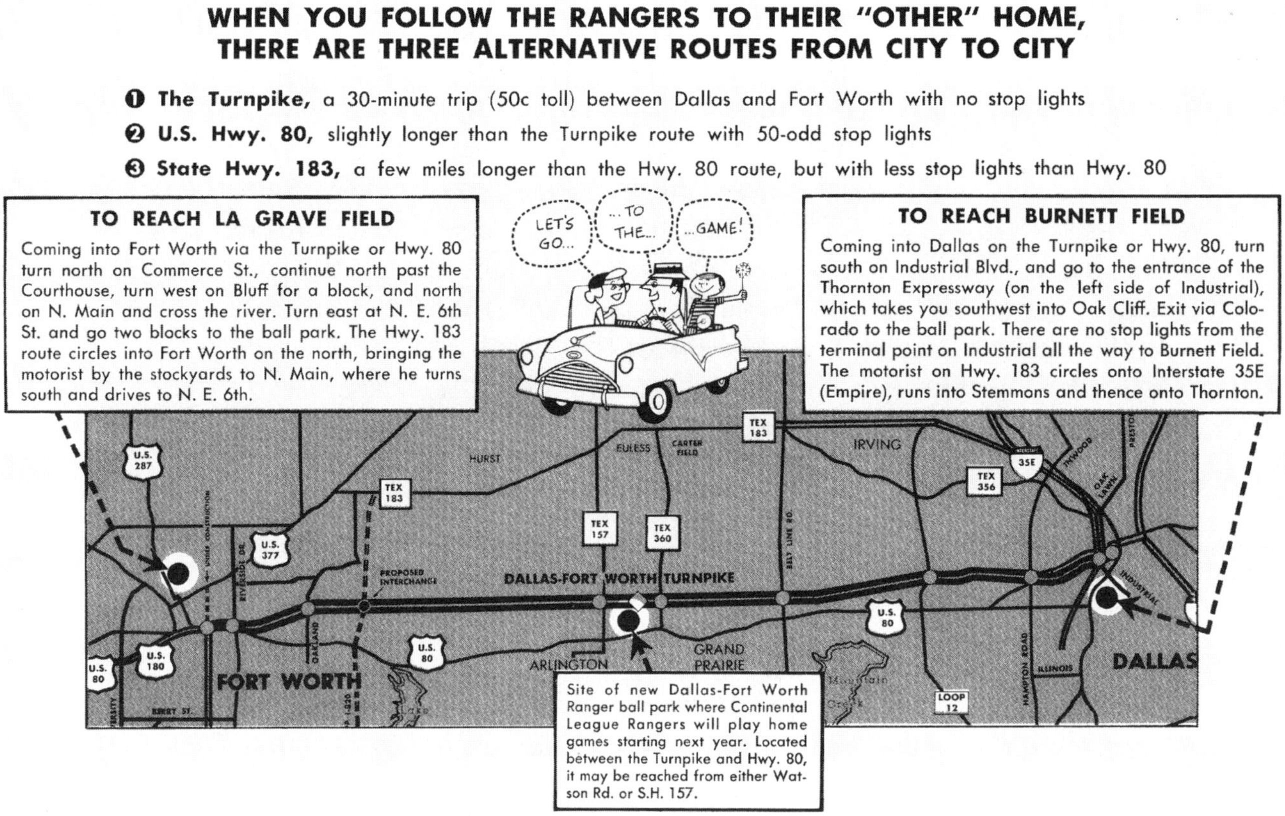

1960 Scorecard map locating LaGrave and Burnett fields (Mark Presswood Collection).

An architect's 1960 rending of the proposed domed stadium in Arlington. Turnpike Stadium—midway between Fort Worth and Dallas—was built in the early 1960s but the dome was not included (AP Wirephoto, Fort Worth Star Telegram*).*

For the 1958 season, the Fort Worth Cats were a farm team of the Chicago Cubs.

Bobby Bragan:

> "It had to be a blow to the city and the team and the fans. The Dodgers were a distinguished franchise. Even during the times in the '50s when many minor leagues began to fail financially, Brooklyn always looked after its own. Dodger minor-league teams traditionally contended for their league titles. The Dodger way of doing things ensured fans would see intelligent, heads-up play from their minor leaguers. The Cubs, however, did not have this reputation and wouldn't have deserved it if they had it. The Cubs were, along with the Philadelphia Phillies, the National League doormat. Their minor-league teams often reflected this. Throughout their organization, the quality of athletes and play was simply much less than that of the Dodgers. The Fort Worth Cats really lost out when they became property of the Cubs."

Mark Presswood:

> "The Fort Worth fans didn't instantly give up on the Cats. They loved baseball, and at least they still had it. And the way the Cats played in their first season as a Cubs farm team didn't hurt, either."

Improbably, the under-new-ownership Cats won the Texas League title for manager Lou Klein. Their 89-64 record didn't recall the glory days of Atz's Cats or the Bragan Bunch, but it was better than any of the other clubs in the league could manage.

The entire team roster was new, of course, with some future Chicago Cubs included. Starting pitchers Bob Anderson and Dick Ellsworth would have reasonably successful big-league careers, as would reliever Ron Perranoski, though ironically the latter's best years would be with the Los Angeles Dodgers. Right fielder Bob Will, infielder Jerry Kindall and catcher Dick Bertell also made it to the majors, and catcher Jim Fanning would later manage both in Fort Worth and the major leagues.

But the big new Cats star was unquestionably a veteran Texas League third baseman named Joe Macko, who had first gained the attention of Fort Worth fans when he played for Dallas. Macko, who slugged 24 homers to lead the Cats in 1957, was like the now-departed Carroll Beringer in that he spent his career doing great things on a minor-league level.

Joe Macko:

> "I spent five years in the Texas League. I think the average player was 25 years old. It was a dead ball league, but I still hit homers, first with Dallas, then Tulsa,

then Dallas again and finally Fort Worth. In one game in Tulsa I hit a ball that went over the fence, a sidewalk behind the fence and broke shingles on the roof of a house behind the sidewalk. The guy who owned the house came to the ballpark the next day and asked if someone would pay to fix his roof.

"The Cats had a reputation with the rest of the teams in the Texas League. Of course they did. It had been because of their tie-in with the Dodgers. The Dodgers knew how to take care of a farm team. The Cats would always have good players, good equipment. On other teams equipment was always a problem. Those teams would maybe give each of us two bats. That was all we got. It was our responsibility afterwards to take care of them. If you broke one, you had to get nails and nail it back together if you could. Afterwards, you'd rub on resin over the nails. No wonder most guys couldn't hit the ball very far.

"You got one uniform for the season, one. If you tore your pants, the team trainer gave you a needle and thread. Today, Juan Gonzalez of the Rangers has twenty pairs of uniform pants in his locker.

"LaGrave Field was kept in top condition. It was beautiful. Spectacular. It wasn't wood, for one thing. All steel. Other places we played were so much rougher. Once, when I played for Dallas, Eddie Knoblauch, our centerfielder, called time because there was a big rattlesnake right where he was trying to play. The guys on our team and the guys from Tulsa, who we were playing, all got our bats, went into the outfield, and we had to find and kill the snake before we could go on playing. Eddie spent the rest of that game looking around the ground at his feet instead of concentrating on the hitters. He thought there were more snakes, and he was right. The next day before the game, workers from the city went out around the outfield fence and killed a bunch of 'em.

"Anyway, those Cats players always seemed to think they were better than the rest of us. When I played for Dallas, we just hated those guys. We had more fights on the field with them than we did with all the other teams in the league put together. And whenever Dallas played Fort Worth at LaGrave, lots of Dallas fans would make the drive to the game. When Fort Worth came to Dallas to play, Cats fans followed along.

"There were fewer minor leagues, but even in the '50s we players figured it took five or six years to make it to the big leagues. We didn't mind staying in the minors for a while. We knew we were there to learn. The minor-league system was designed for that.

"Fort Worth was a good place for me to play. I was married and living in Dallas, so I could drive to games. It was a nice drive, an easy drive. Hell, when I first started in pro ball I had the extra job of driving my team's bus. No kidding. I'd signed with the Indians and was just starting out in their farm system. George Susce was my team manager. One day George tells us all to put on old clothes because we're going to play a series in Batavia. I was the team bus driver because in high shcool I'd had a part-time job driving a beer truck. So the club gave me $50 extra a month to drive the bus. Big money, that was. Important money. Susce tells me as we set off to drive

100 miles and stop the bus. I do. He tells the other players to get out and run the next mile ahead of the bus. Nobody dares say no. The manager wrote regular reports on everybody and sent them to the big shots. Attitude was a big part of those reports. So everybody but the manager, the coaches and me gets out and runs a mile. Then 100 miles later we stop and they all get out to run again. Think ballplayers today would do that?

"Well, you wanted to play for the Fort Worth Cats because they did everything first-class, including food on those occasions the ballclub was supposed to feed you. Minor-league players usually ate pretty bad. We knew nothing about good nutrition anyway. It was said that if you went to spring training with the Dodgers, even if you were on one of their minor-league rosters, at dinner you got two or three choices of meats. Incredible. In '54, I was loaned to the Cincinnati Reds with maybe five days to go in their spring training. I got there and found breakfast was buffet style and very bad—rye toast, a cup of lousy coffee, powdered eggs and grits. I figured lunch would be better, but we got an apple, two pieces of stale bread with one piece of bologna in between and a small cup of milk. The milk was sour. Okay, I thought, dinner has to be an improvement. Well, I got one pork chop with an inch of fat all around it. There was one ice cream scoop of mashed potatoes and the potatoes ran over the side of the plate because they were mixed so thin.

"But in Fort Worth, even though it was the Cubs rather than the Dodgers, the way players got treated was still better than anywhere else, I think. The Cats players stuck together. There was real camaraderie. I think that happened on major-league and minor-league teams in those days. When the Fort Worth Cats traveled, say, to San Antonio, we went by train. After the ballgame we would go out together to find a grocery store that was still open. We'd pool our money and buy a loaf of bread, some lunch meat, and fix ourselves sandwiches. Then we'd sit around eating them and talking baseball all night long. It was fun. It brought teams together.

"Players could make up for low salaries because local merchants took care of you. Fort Worth was famous for that. Pawnshop owners there sold us stuff extra cheap. There was a barbecue place where the owner was a fan, and he'd invite players over to eat. No charge.

"You learned where to go on road trips, too. I remember Bishop's Restaurant in Tulsa. We always ate a lot of White Castle hamburgers, too, ten for a dollar. Two bites and one of those hamburgers was gone, but they were cheap.

"With the Cats, places would give you a few gallons of gas or milk for home runs or pitching victories. A lot of players didn't have cars, but the gas was something you could give to the family you were boarding with. You always wanted to pay them back for being nice. I heard that once Joe Landrum, a pitcher for the Cats, painted the house of the family he was staying with.

"We didn't give 'em the milk, though. That, we drank ourselves as soon as we got it."

The 1957 season saw several colorful players join Texas League teams. No newcomer, though, was more colorful than Harry "The Hat" Walker, a former National League batting champion who arrived in the Texas League as player-manager of the Houston Buffs.

Harry Walker:

> "I loved the Texas League. Everybody loved the Texas League. I loved Texas itself, loved Houston, still love Houston even though the fans there got on me some later when I managed the Astros in the National League. And when I managed in Houston for the first time, with the Buffs and not the Astros, who didn't even exist then, my team would come to Fort Worth to play and I loved being there. Their infield dirt was black. Looked fine. What I remember about the Fort Worth fans is that they knew their baseball. They would support their home team, but they would also cheer for opposing players who did something good. Fort Worth fans came to watch baseball, not like fans today who spend more time looking at the scoreboard ads than the players."

The Cats front office continued to cater to fans with special events before and after games. Comedian Jackie Price was a favorite entertainer. His pregame act included shooting a baseball into the air from a bazooka, jumping in a jeep, driving to the place where he thought the ball would come down and catching it before it hit the ground. Price also would hang by his knees upside down in the batting cage and swing at and hit pitched balls.

Joe Macko:

> "The games at LaGrave would often feature entertainment besides baseball. For a while Vaughn Monroe, the band leader, went out on the minor-league circuit. He had a gal named Dagmar who was his singer. She was, as we said in those days, stacked. Well, they performed at LaGrave and 10,000 fans pushed into the stands. Dagmar had this act where she always sang a love song to a player. I got picked for her to sing to, and I told Al Panzera, the photographer from the *Star-Telegram*, to get ready. You see, I got some teeth knocked out earlier in my career. Ground ball or something. I played the next day. Anyway, I had false teeth, a bridge, and when Dagmar sang to me, put her arms around me and everything, I turned away for a second, turned back around, and yanked out my false teeth. It was hilarious. Everybody but Dagmar laughed so hard they couldn't stand up."

In 1958, the Cats hosted the Texas League All-Star game at LaGrave Field. Fort Worth beat the rest of the league's best 5-3. But that win and the regular season title had to satisfy the team and its fans; Austin eliminated Fort Worth in the first round of the post-season play-offs.

Jim Snyder, 1963 second baseman for the Dallas-Fort Worth Rangers (Special Collections, UTA).

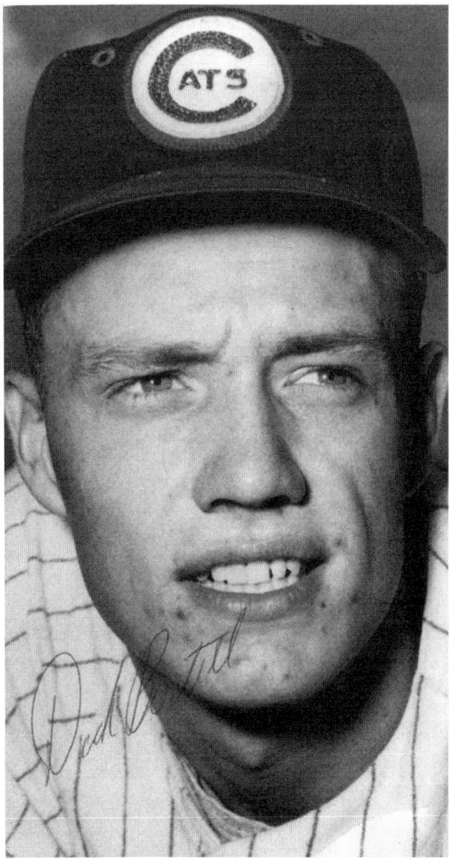

Dick Bertell, 1958 (Mark Presswood Collection).

No one realized it, but the Fort Worth Cats would never finish first again.

Almost as unthinkable was the decision by team ownership in 1959 to move the Cats from the Double-A Texas League to the Triple-A American Association.

Mark Presswood:

> "In 1959, management at both Dallas and Fort Worth decided it was time to move up in league classification. Certainly Double-A as a Cubs' farm club wasn't the same as Double-A with the Dodgers. The Cubs supported the Cats moving from the Texas League. Lou Klein came back as the Cats' manager, the first guy since Bobby Bragan to manage the team more than just one season. Klein had a pretty good team he took into Triple-A."

Several players—Macko, Will, Kindall, Bertell and Ellsworth—joined their manager for a second season with the Cats. Future major leaguers Seth Morehead and Dick Drott were added to the team, and future Cubs Hall of Fame outfielder Billy Williams was a late-season addition. Still, competition at the Triple-A level was tougher. The Cats' 81-81 record placed them second in the American Association's Western Division. Under their new play-off format, that entitled Fort Worth to take on Eastern Division champ, the Louisville Redbirds, in the first round. Louisville had dominated American Association regular-season play, winning over 100 games. Still, the Redbirds were swept in four straight games by the Cats, who then lost the season championship play-off to Minneapolis, four games to three.

Though the Cats' first season in the American Association had been reasonably successful, the team was about to undergo radical change. Major league geography was involved again, this time big-league expansion. Fort Worth was about to lose its beloved Cats, and, in one sense, the villain was the same man who'd brought so much to the team for so long —Branch Rickey.

After leaving the Pittsburgh Pirates, Rickey rejoined the St. Louis Cardinals but did not become a controlling force on the team. Rickey, who had broken the major-league "color barrier" and completely restructured the minor leagues, left St. Louis to concentrate with attorney William Shea on a new plan—a third professional major league to be known as the Continental League, one that would place its franchises in big cities lacking major-league baseball teams. Demand was certainly there. Shea had originally been hired by the mayor of New York to find a way to bring National League baseball back to the city. Fans all over the country tuned in to televised major-league games every Saturday. The Northeast no longer contained the only cities big enough to support big-league clubs financially. Every national survey indicated the South and West were the regions where the most explosive population growth could be anticipated.

Rickey's bold pronouncements about his new league provided the existing National and American leagues with a virtual road map for their own expansion. Rickey believed New York City would support a new team, that Houston would, that Minneapolis was ready for top-flight baseball and that California could support several more big-league teams.

Owners of the existing major-league clubs acted quickly. The Washington Senators had, for too long, been the worst team in the American League. Fans in the nation's capitol were demonstrably uninterested in the club. So it was announced that the Senators would move to Minneapolis-St. Paul in 1961 and be re-named the Minnesota Twins. Then two new expansion clubs would begin play, their rosters stocked by drafting some veterans from current major-league rosters but mostly with some of the best prospects from existing teams' minor-league systems. One of these clubs would be known as the Los Angeles Angels. O'Malley felt the Angels would be to his better-established Dodgers what the old Brooklyn franchise had been to the Yankees—clearly second-best in terms of attention from a home city. The other American League expansion team would replace the Senators in Washington and take the Senators' name, too. The hope was that fans in the D.C. area would better support a struggling new team than a struggling familiar one.

Major-league expansion did not stop with the American League, either. In 1962 the National League also expanded to ten teams. Its new clubs would be placed in New York and Houston.

Bobby Bragan:

"That was really it for the Cats right there, though it would take a few more years. You knew that if Houston got a major-league team, leaders in the Dallas-Fort Worth area would demand a major-league team, too. This is the mindset of sports fans. They will support minor-league play until they believe somebody else in the region or state is getting better sports entertainment on a major-league level. What recently had been perfectly satisfactory baseball to Fort Worth and Dallas fans would instantly become second-rate the moment Houston fans got to see big leaguers, got to see Mays and Clemente and Aaron.

"Some places in Texas like Beaumont and San Antonio were not ever going to get major-league teams, so their minor-league clubs could continue to operate decently. But Fort Worth-Dallas? Those fans knew they had every bit as much right as Houston to enjoy major-league baseball. And they began to holler for it."

Attendence in Fort Worth and Dallas had been down anyway in 1959. Fans could stay home and watch games on TV now. There were movie theaters, more stores, and pro football was about to arrive with the Dallas Cowboys.

Bob Bluthardt:

"By the '60s, of course, the major-league world just got bigger. The entertainment world did, too. There were more things for people to do. For many, getting out and doing something for yourself, like going to a game at LaGrave Field, became less attractive than the packaged reality of staying home and staring at a TV screen. For Cats fans in the '20s, '30s, even the '40s, how many other entertainment options were there? But this had changed.

"We simply cannot underestimate the impact televised major-league baseball had on the minor leagues."

Team ownership in Fort Worth and Dallas did the previously unthinkable: they merged the long-time rivals.

Mark Presswood:

"It was a financial necessity. All minor-league teams were struggling. Amon Carter, Jr., led the way in Fort Worth to put the two teams together. The new Dallas-Fort Worth Rangers would play one home series at LaGrave and the next home series at Burnett Park in Dallas. This new club signed on with the Los Angeles Angels, the American League expansion club, which pretty much guaranteed the Rangers weren't going to be much good. Another important point is that baseball expansion not only thinned out the talent in the big leagues, it also watered down the quality of play in the minors, because some of the average players on the expansion team rosters would have been the top players on minor-league teams."

Ranger management tried to retain Cats' fans loyalty by appointing former Fort Worth player Jim Fanning as manager. A few "name" players dotted the team's roster, including Don Larsen, who'd pitched a perfect game in the World Series, and fringe-level major-league veterans Mel Wright and Ray Jablonski. Otherwise, the Dallas-Fort Worth roster was packed with questionable hitters and pitchers the Angels had signed to stock their minor-league system prior to their formal expansion draft to begin major-league play in 1961. And, predictably, the team was terrible. It finished eighth in the American Association with a 64-90 record.

Just as predictably, Fort Worth fans usually chose to stay home instead of going out to LaGrave. They didn't like Dallas' hated name coming before Fort Worth's on team jerseys. They really disliked the poor quality of play they saw on those rare occasions they did make it out to the ballpark.

But the Dallas-Fort Worth Rangers lasted a few more seasons. In 1961, new manager Walker Cooper actually enjoyed the services of some good young players, mostly youngsters plucked by the Angels in the major-league expansion draft and farmed out for a year's pro baseball experience before being hurried on to the big leagues. Dean Chance and Jim Fregosi both went on to become established stars. Chuck Tanner was a less distinguished player, but he later managed the Pittsburgh Pirates to a World Series victory. The '61 Rangers finished fifth in the American Association with a 72-77 record.

By 1962, the American Association itself was in trouble. With major-league teams now all over the country, there was no region a minor league could truly consider exclusively its own. Only six teams, including the Dallas-Fort Worth Rangers, were left in the American Association when the '62 season got underway. Dallas-Fort Worth was clearly the worst of these. Though future big leaguers Cookie Rojas and Sammy Ellis were on the roster, overall the team could only crawl home with a 59-90 mark. Fort Worth fans were especially disdainful. One game at LaGrave matching the Rangers against Denver drew only 476 fans. Though doubleheaders had always drawn big crowds in Fort Worth, a Denver-Rangers twin bill attracted just 557 paying customers. Worse, those three Denver games were the Rangers' last LaGrave Field games of the season. Clearly, Fort Worth fans had completely lost interest in them.

The American Association folded following the 1962 season. Somehow, the Dallas-Fort Worth Rangers hung on. The team affiliated with the Minnesota Twins and, improbably, was accepted into the remnants of the Pacific Coast League. With road trips to far-off places like San Diego instead of Waco or Houston, Fort Worth fans no longer could conveniently follow their team wherever it might play.

If they'd still cared enough, Fort Worth fans might have enjoyed watching the '63 Rangers play at LaGrave. Unlike the Angels, Minnesota was about to become an American League powerhouse. As had been the case when the Dodgers were aligned with the Cats, future major-league stars again called LaGrave Field home for a season. César Tovar became a Dallas-Fort Worth Ranger, and so did a Cuban refugee named Pedro Oliva. Later, he'd call himself Tony, and win several major league batting titles. Even the 1963 Dallas-Fort Worth manager was distinguished. Jack McKeon would go on to a long career as a big-league manager and general manager. In 1999, he still skippered the Cincinnati Reds. McKeon led the Rangers to a 79-79 record but wasn't able to convince enough people to come out to LaGrave Field. Attendence was dismal. Dallas-Fort Worth team owners were thoroughly disenchanted.

Enter Fort Worth's Tommy Mercer.

Mark Presswood:

> "Mercer believed that Fort Worth would still support a team if fans felt it was their own team. None of this half-Fort Worth, half-Dallas business. He acquired the ballclub and immediately placed them back in the Texas League. The club's 1964 motto was 'The Cats Are Back!' Mercer was even able to put together a new working agreement with the Chicago Cubs. What he couldn't do was get a good team on the field, or get fans to believe it was really just like the old days again.
>
> "Dallas stayed on in the Pacific Coast League. The Cats dropped back from Triple-A to Double-A. Mercer acted as Cats general manager, and he hired Alex Grammas, a former big-league infielder, as Cats manager. The stars of the team were shortstop Don Kessinger, catcher John Felske, and pitcher Billy Connors."

Mercer tried hard. He convinced Lamar Hunt, whose other sports interests included ownership of the Kansas City Chiefs pro football team, to join him as a limited partner. There were special events at LaGrave throughout the season, though the venerable old park was showing signs of age in cracking paint and creaky plumbing. But the Fort Worth Cats had lost their magic. The team's 51-89 was the worst in the Texas League; the Cats finished 34 games out of first place.

The Fort Worth Cats' last home games at LaGrave Field were played against the Tulsa Oilers. The first contest was a success on the field and at the box office; 3,638 fans watched the Cats beat Tulsa 7-1. Bob Flynn pitched a three-hitter for Fort Worth; Felske clubbed a homer off losing pitcher Steve Carlton, a future Hall-of-Famer. The next night the Cats lost

3-2; sportswriter Frank Luksa told readers "normalcy returned to LaGrave Field." There was supposed to be a third game in the series, but it was rained out.

The Cats then left to conclude the 1964 season in Tulsa. On September 7, they closed their year by splitting a doubleheader with the Oilers. Fort Worth won the first game 5-3 and lost the second 1-0. Afterwards, Mercer told reporters that "with the help of the Chicago Cubs, we hope to improve the baseball situation in Fort Worth with a winning team." Cats' players and their manager were equally hopeful.

"The fans were very patient and understanding," Grammas told reporters. "It's a credit to the whole city, and it makes you want to come back. We weren't afraid to show up at the park, and I can't say the same for other places I have played."

"[We've] got great people to play for," infielder Frank DeMoss agreed. "It's a shame they couldn't have had a winner. They certainly deserve one."

They never had another chance, at least with the Fort Worth Cats. Within weeks, it was announced that Dallas would return to the Texas League, link with Fort Worth again, and the Dallas-Fort Worth Spurs would begin play in 1965.

Bobby Bragan:

"When they were brought back to town in 1964, it was already too late for the Fort Worth Cats. Relationships between teams and the cities they represent are like great love affairs. For a time, they're wonderful, but when they're over, they're over. The attention of Fort Worth baseball fans had been turned elsewhere.

"I know something about this. Remember, I managed the Milwaukee Braves during their last season in that city and stayed with the team when it moved to Atlanta in 1966. Now, when the Braves came to town in 1953 the fans took them to their hearts. By the time the team departed twelve seasons later, people weren't coming out to the ballpark anymore. Why? What happened? I was there, and I'm still not sure I can say.

"What I do know about the demise of the Cats is that the most influential people in Fort Worth were no longer committed to the team. They wanted to join with Dallas leaders and bring major-league baseball to the area. This is what they talked up at Rotary Club meetings, at Lions Club meetings, when they made speeches to area chambers of commerce and business groups. 'We must have major league baseball' was their intention and their message.

"So they brought the Fort Worth and Dallas minor-league clubs back together again and built a new stadium in which that hybrid team could play. Turnpike Stadium, they called it, and built it in Arlington. They were thinking ahead; if a

> major-league franchise could be lured to this area, it could play in Turnpike Stadium, which was more or less equidistant from downtown Fort Worth and downtown Dallas."

The Spurs affiliated with, in order, the Chicago Cubs (1965-1967), the Houston Astros (1968), and the Baltimore Orioles (1969-1971). They remained in Turnpike Stadium through the 1971 season. The Orioles were a dominant major-league team during much of this period, and Spurs' rosters reflected it: Bobby Grich and Don Baylor played for the Spurs. For a while, Cal Ripken, Sr., was the team's manager.

The Spurs were never anything but a holding pattern, however. Local leaders, led by Tom Vandergriff of Arlington, aggressively sought out owners of major-league teams whose clubs were struggling at the ticket window. It first seemed Charles O. Finley might move his Kansas City A's to Turnpike Stadium, but in 1968 Finley cut a deal with Oakland, California, instead. Undaunted, Vandergriff and company turned their attentions to another lowly American League franchise.

Mark Presswood:

> "Bob Short wanted to get out of Washington, D.C. Coming to Texas looked good to him. He worked out a deal with Vandergriff. Charlie Finley decided to get in the way. He told Short he wanted the Senators to give outfielder Jeff Burroughs to the A's in exchange for Finley's vote supporting the Washington move to Arlington. But Short got enough votes from other owners to avoid that."

With major-league officials in favor of the Washington Senators moving South to become the Texas Rangers, it only remained for Commissioner Bowie Kuhn to work out the details. To sort things out and reach an agreement between the major-league owners and Mercer and Hunt, the owners of the displaced minor-league Dallas-Fort Worth Spurs, he called in the president of the Texas League, Bobby Bragan.

Bobby Bragan:

> "This was a sad duty for me. The Spurs were not the Cats, not any semblence of the Cats, and yet they retained at least a small percentage of the rich Fort Worth Cats tradition. This Fort Worth-Dallas territory snatch occurred about one year after I assumed the Texas League presidency. Kuhn summoned me to New York with Mercer and Hunt, the object being to work out a reasonable indemnity to be paid by the collective major-league owners to both Mercer and Hunt and to the Texas League team owners whose investments would also be affected by the situation.

"After much discussion, the Texas League was awarded $640,000—$360,000 to Mercer and Hunt and $40,000 apiece to each of the other seven franchises. The eighth spot in the Texas League then went to Midland. The Washington Senators became the Texas Rangers. Beginning in 1972, baseball fans in Fort Worth watched their favorite sport at the renamed Arlington Stadium.

"If major-league baseball isn't careful, it will completely eradicate the minors. And the major leagues need the minor leagues. Even with continuous expansion diluting major-league rosters, if clubs intend to charge top dollar for admission they must provide paying customers with entertaining games played by knowledgeable professionals—and baseball knowledge comes from instruction in the minor leagues."

Harry Walker:

"The minor leagues can give extra chances to players who can become superstars if only they have the opportunity. Some say we don't need the minor leagues anymore. I tell 'em that without the minors, we never would have heard of Stan Musial. Musial was signed by the Cardinals as a pitcher, but he hurt his arm. Today he'd get released. But back then a St. Louis farm club needed an extra outfielder, and Stan always could hit. He got sent there, hit about a million, and became one of the greatest stars of all time. No minor leagues, and Stan is back in Pennsylvania coal country where he came from."

Hank Aaron:

"They talk about dismantling the minor leagues. I think that would be the saddest thing in the world for baseball. Players today don't know the fundamentals, the little things you do in a game to help you win.

"The Fort Worth Cats showed the way it still should be done. Players were taught how to steal, to bunt, to hit and to run. Why do you think for all those years the Dodgers, Yankees and Cardinals had the best records in the major leagues? It was because they used their minor-league teams as places for their future players to learn to play baseball right. But that's over now."

Carroll Beringer:

"I guess it's wrong to sit around now and say things aren't as good as they used to be. But I don't think there's anything wrong with my saying this: Every day here in Fort Worth I meet somebody who tells me what the Fort Worth Cats used to mean to him, and I tell him right back what the Fort Worth fans used to mean to us. It was a special time and team and place to play, and all of us who shared that time are so glad we did."

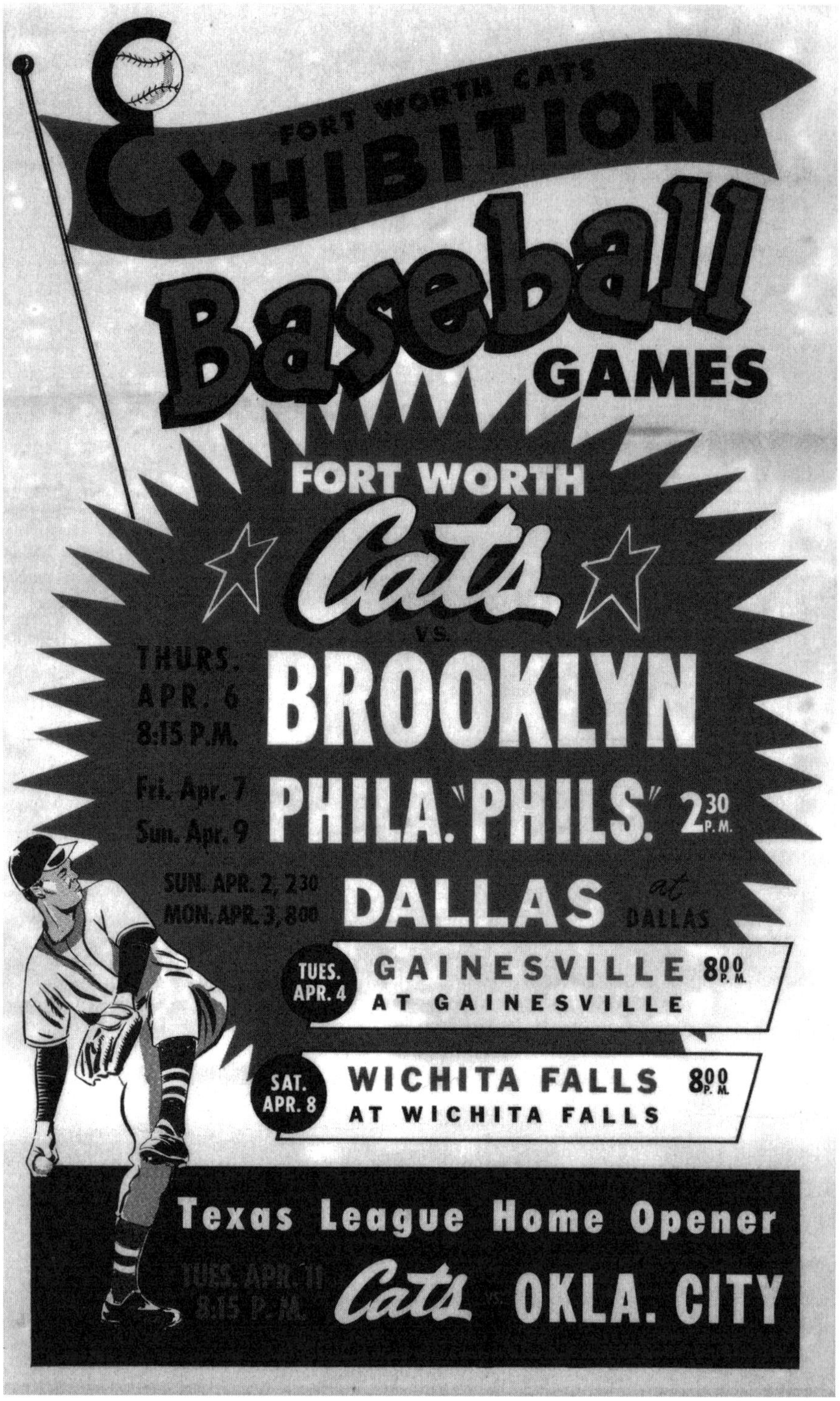

1951 (Bobby Bragan Collection).

Afterword

During the spring of 1999, discussion began in earnest between Fort Worth city officials and a group of baseball fans and business leaders who wanted to rebuild LaGrave Field. The plan was the same as it had been for years—add a Fort Worth Cats franchise to the Texas-Louisiana League as LaGrave's official home team and supplement that club's games with those hosted by Carroll Beringer's beloved Texas Wesleyan University.

It may just happen. Fort Worth has focused on fixing up its historic North Side stockyards to attract tourists; a rebuilt LaGrave Field would link the stockyards and downtown. Bobby Bragan has proposed a baseball museum as an add on, with his own career memorabilia on permanent loan. Texas-Lousiana League officials are enthusiastic; like the Texas League pioneers more than a century ago, they welcome new franchises from any city apparently willing and able to support them.

No one expects a new LaGrave Field and Fort Worth Cats baseball team to duplicate in quality what came before. The concept is to celebrate the past, not to mourn it. The new Cats would have to provide family entertainment at reasonable prices to draw sufficient fans to the ballpark. As Bobby Bragan has always insisted, fans need to believe the team they support can, at least once in a while, win it all.

For a while, a long while, the original Fort Worth Cats did exactly that. They were part of an old-time baseball world that brought players and fans together for quality baseball recreation, community pride and occasional ice-cream socials in someone's backyard. The Cats exemplified an era when playing baseball meant fun more than finance, when signing autographs for fans was an honor instead of an obligation.

So no new team, no rebuilt stadium can make all that happen again. But so long as there is the possibility of some continued tradition, some simple, baseball-generated pleasure back on the banks of the Trinity River, the same fans who once loved the Cats will continue to hope they'll hear a one-time motto in Fort Worth again:

"The Cats are back."

Index